THE MORAL LIFE

OLIVER A. JOHNSON
University of California, Riverside

London
GEORGE ALLEN AND UNWIN LTD
RUSKIN HOUSE · MUSEUM STREET

FIRST PUBLISHED IN 1969

This book is copyright under the Berne Convention. All rights are reserved. Apart from any fair dealing for the purpose of private study, research, criticism or review, as permitted under the Copyright Act, 1956, no part of this publication may be reproduced, stored in a retrieval system, or transmitted, in any form or by any means, electronic, electrical, chemical, mechanical, optical, photocopying recording or otherwise, without the prior permission of the copyright owner. Enquiries should be addressed to the Publishers.

© *George Allen & Unwin Ltd.*, 1969
SBN 04 170023 6

PRINTED IN GREAT BRITAIN
in 11 *on* 13*pt Baskerville*
BY ABERDEEN UNIVERSITY PRESS

To Julie, Stuart, Elizabeth and Melinda

PREFACE

Several years ago I undertook to write a book on the problem of moral knowledge. At the time that I began work on that book I was disposed to believe that our moral beliefs, to the extent that they were defensible, could be justified by an appeal to a kind of intellectual intuition. The more I considered the objections to such a view, however, the more convinced I became that it would not do. Led by this conviction into a study and appraisal of alternative theories of moral knowledge, I was finally forced to conclude that none of the other solutions to the problem, either traditional or contemporary, was any more satisfactory than intuitionism. Having rejected them all, I found myself facing the decision to become an ethical sceptic or to find a new way in which to support moral beliefs. Being reluctant to accept the defeat that my embracing scepticism would imply, I made an attempt to move in the other direction. In the concluding chapters of the book I sketched, in a very tentative form, a new approach to the problem of moral knowledge that I believed could in principle meet the objections to traditional views. At the time I recognized that the theory I had drafted was insufficient and in many ways unsatisfactory. So in my Preface to the book I wrote, 'The conclusions I reach could probably best be described as prolegomena to the elaboration of a theory of ethics. I have plans, which I hope will be realized in the next few years, of elaborating such a theory.' This book is the realization of those plans.

I have been assisted in writing *The Moral Life* by a grant from the Humanities Institute of the University of California. I wish to express my grateful appreciation to the University for this grant. The manuscript itself was written in two places, the British Museum and the Bromley (Kent) Public Library. I should like to thank the staffs of both libraries for their consideration, cooperation, and assistance to me in this task. I appreciate also the very helpful suggestions and criticisms made to me by Professors H. D. Lewis and Norman Richardson and by Dr A. C. Ewing, all of whom read drafts of the manuscript. Finally, I owe my greatest debt of gratitude to my family, whose contributions to the book, although spread throughout its pages, are mostly invisible to all eyes except my own.

Riverside, California
May 1969

I

IF someone were to ask me 'Do you want to live a moral life?' I should unhesitatingly answer 'Yes'. Indeed, who wouldn't? The ideal is a laudable one that almost everyone espouses – as long as it remains unspecified. But when we drop our sights from the abstract to the concrete, to the decisions we must make and the actions we must perform in our everyday life if we are to live morally, we encounter difficulties on every hand. We find we must do things that we do not want to do, make sacrifices that we would prefer to avoid. We soon discover that it is very hard to put into practice what we have preached.

Because we find the demands of the moral life to be onerous, it is only natural that we should look for ways of escaping them. When someone tells us that it is our duty to do a certain act but we want very much to do something else instead, we shall, unless we are unusually docile, offer him some resistance. It may be only to find excuses for avoiding our responsibility or it may be to present reasons against, and to demand that he provide reasons in favour of our fulfilling it. At least we ask: '*Why* ought I to do the act you say is my duty?' Anyone who seriously faces a conflict between what he feels or is told he ought to do and what he would like to do is bound to raise such a question. When he does so, he transforms his problem from a practical into a theoretical issue and becomes, at least for the moment, a moral philosopher. For high among the essential concerns of moral philosophy is the task of finding an answer to the question 'Why ought people to act morally?' – if such an answer can be found at all.

Most moral philosophers have recognized as much. As a result they have usually divided their interests into an attempt, first, to develop a theory of the moral life (that is, to say how men ought, as moral beings, to act) and, secondly, to defend their theory, by explaining why men ought to act in the ways it lays down. And often they have devoted more attention to the second than to the first of these tasks. For it is by far the harder to accomplish. Indeed, the history of moral philosophy down to the present time seems to indicate that the problem it poses is insoluble. The difficulty can be put, in its simplest terms, in the following way: Most of us believe that we ought to live morally, that we have a duty to act in certain ways and to refrain from acting in others. But can we provide any good reasons in support of this belief? Can we *justify* the moral 'ought' and, if so, how? Or is it finally incapable of justification?

In this essay I shall attempt to answer these questions. Before I commence on that task, however, I should first explain some of the reasons that have driven many moral philosophers, particularly in the present day, to the conclusion that it is impossible to justify our moral beliefs. This will require a brief review of the main traditions in Western ethics. Since my purpose in this review is to trace the arguments that have led philosophers to the conclusion that the moral 'ought' cannot be justified, perhaps the best place for me to begin is at the end – in the twentieth century – because it contains what I believe to be the strongest challenge that has yet been raised against the possibility of our providing any arguments capable of justifying our beliefs about how we ought to act. The challenge, which has been stated in its most pointed form by the British philosopher H. A. Prichard, may at first glance seem innocuous; such an appearance, however, is deceptive for it is in truth capable of devastating traditional moral philosophy. The case against the tradition rests on a single statement: 'An "ought", if it is to be derived at all, can only be derived from another "ought".'[1]

I believe that this short if somewhat mystifying pronouncement destroys most of the arguments that moral philosophers have in the past employed to justify their conclusions about how we ought to act. It does so by the simple but thoroughly effective device of implying that the arguments they have advanced in support of their conclusions are and must be logically untenable. To see how it accomplishes this result, we must examine its implications. Since I am convinced that any theory of the moral life, if it is to stand a chance of success, must meet the objections implicit in this statement, it would be wise, before I embark on such a theory, to be clear about what the statement means, what it implies, and just why its critique of traditional moral philosophy is so effective. At least five questions can be raised concerning it. (1) What does it mean? (2) Is it true? (3) What are its implications? (4) Do these eliminate moral philosophy as a legitimate discipline or can a theory of moral obligation be developed which succeeds in circumventing them? (5) If the latter, what must such a theory be? I shall deal with the first three questions briefly, mainly in Part I; my attempt to answer the last two questions will occupy the remainder of the essay.

What does the cryptic dictum 'An "ought" can be derived only from another "ought"' mean?[2] The critical terms in it are 'ought' and 'derived', and both require explanation. The essential point concerning the term 'ought' is that it refers to a distinctively moral concept – the 'ought' of moral obligation. It is the concept we use when we talk moral language, when we make such statements as 'I ought to be just in my dealings with my fellow-men' or 'I ought not to inflict gratuitous pain on others'. In his statement, thus, Prichard is concerned with the same issue with which we have begun – the problem of justifying the moral 'ought'. He is maintaining that such an 'ought' can be justified only by an appeal to another moral 'ought'.

The term 'derived', on the other hand, stands for a logical concept. It is concerned with the question of the reasons we give in support of our beliefs about what we ought to do and the connection between these reasons and those beliefs. If someone were to challenge our conviction regarding the duty to be just, for example, asking '*Why* ought I to act justly?' he would in effect be demanding that we offer some argument capable of convincing him that this conviction is true. Any argument that we may give in reply, if it is to be cogent, must, as a minimum condition, be logically valid. The conclusion that we are trying to establish must follow logically from the premises we offer in its support for, unless it does, we cannot legitimately 'derive' it from them. With its two crucial concepts thus understood, the meaning of the statement 'An "ought" can be derived only from another "ought"' can be elaborated as follows: When we attempt to provide reasons in support of our convictions about how we ought to act, the reasons we give, if they are to do the job required, must include among them one that contains a moral 'ought' or, in other words, states a moral conviction.

Is the contention that an 'ought' can be derived only from another 'ought' true? Or, to put the question in a more manageable form: What arguments can be advanced in its support and how strong are these arguments? The important point to recognize here is that Prichard rests his case on *logical* rather than on ethical considerations. His thesis that an 'ought' can be derived only from another 'ought' is simply an application to ethics of the basic principle of logic that, if an argument is to be valid, every concept that appears in its conclusion must appear somewhere in its premises as well. Is this logical principle true? Occasionally philosophers have tried to deny it but none of their efforts has proved notably successful. For any such attempt leads one inevitably into contradiction. We must, I think, grant the principle to be incontrovertible; therefore we have to agree that, if we employ any argument in support of our moral convictions, we must be sure that we do not insert an 'ought' into our conclusion for which no logical provision has been made in our premises. Otherwise our argument will have no cogency.

The significance of the contention that an 'ought' can be derived only from another 'ought' lies in its implications, which are profound and disturbing. To appreciate them we must turn back briefly to look at the Western tradition of moral philosophy. From the time of the Greeks ethicists have been concerned with finding solutions to man's practical moral problems; one of the main tasks they have set themselves has been to answer the question 'How ought we, as moral beings, to act and live?' The classical answers that have been given are well-known to every initiate in philosophy – the doctrine of the Golden Mean, the Categorical Imperative, the Principle of Utility, and many others. But it is not enough for an ethicist to lay down a rule to govern moral conduct; as a philosopher he has the responsibility of providing arguments on behalf of his rule. He must, therefore, attempt to answer a second question: 'Why ought we to act according to the rule that has been laid down or, for that matter, according to any rule?' And, as I have already said, this second question is incomparably more difficult to answer satisfactorily than the first. Indeed, most of the arguments that traditional ethicists have offered in support of their rules of moral conduct cannot bear critical scrutiny. I shall not attempt to review these at length here but shall limit myself to a brief examination of a few main types of theory; most of the major writers in the tradition exemplify one of these types.

The problem that the moral philosophers have faced, and with which we are now concerned, can be formulated in the following terms: The object is to provide an argument from whose premises we can legitimately conclude that men have a moral obligation to act in some specified manner. What should the nature of that argument be? To what kind of premises should we appeal in support of our moral conclusion? Historically, one of the main ways of coping with this problem has been by an attempt to integrate ethics with some other intellectual discipline. If certain propositions from the other discipline are true, then the rule of moral action stipulated must be true as well, since its truth follows from theirs. The ethical problem can thus be solved by establishing the truth of propositions that are themselves non-ethical in nature. The type of non-ethical discipline chosen for this purpose has varied through history. In the Middle Ages, for example, theology was favoured. Moral philosophers defined our duties in terms of the will of God. Both to determine how we ought to act and to support the conclusion that it was truly our duty to act in this way, they had only to discover what God willed. An answer to the theological question carried with it an answer to the ethical. In recent centuries theology has largely given way to science as a foundation for ethics. To discover how we ought to act, according to many contemporary moral philosophers, we must turn to biology, or physics, or sociology, or psychology, or simply to 'science'.

However much these two types of ethical justification may seem to differ from each other, they share one crucial assumption – that the arguments used in support of a conclusion about how we ought to act may be non-ethical in character. Unfortunately, this assumption is untenable. Over two hundred years ago, in a famous passage in his *Treatise of Human Nature*, David Hume pointed out that it is impossible to derive an 'ought' from an 'is'. The case for his thesis is simple and convincing. Elaborated, Hume's argument holds that no set of purely descriptive premises – whether they describe what God wills, what science has discovered, what the state decrees, what public opinion favours, or anything else – can logically support a conclusion that asserts a moral 'ought'. Separating the premises from the conclusion is a chasm that no logic can leap.

Although his argument revealed with devastating clarity the logical impossibility of justifying our beliefs about how we ought to act by an appeal to 'facts' of any kind, Hume was by no means the first moral philosopher to recognize the independent status of ethical propositions. Rather a strong tradition, with its roots in Greek philosophy, has reiterated the thesis that ethics is a unique discipline whose normative propositions are different in kind and underivable from propositions of any other sort. Having cut the logical ties between ethics and all other disciplines, such philosophers are faced with the very difficult task of finding some rational support for their normative propositions. Traditionally, they have solved this problem in either one of two quite different ways. On one side are the axiologists, who first argue that the normative propositions of ethics must be divided into two types, those which assert values and those which assert moral obligations, and then go on to conclude that the latter can be derived from the former. Utilitarianism (in the broad rather than narrow sense) offers perhaps the best example of such an axiological mode of ethical argument. To decide what we ought to do, the utilitarians contend, we must turn to the consequences of our acts, choosing to do that act which will produce the greatest possible amount of good.

As a theory of the moral life, utilitarianism runs into difficulties in two places. First, it must find some way of supporting the value propositions from which it derives its conclusions about how we ought to act. For, unless these can be supported, we have no reason for believing that the consequences of any act we might do would be better than those of some alternative act, hence have no grounds for deciding which of several alternative acts we might do is the one we ought to do. To accomplish his goal, therefore, the utilitarian must provide us with a basis for making relative evaluations. He can do this if he is able to justify as true at least one proposition that asserts a value; i.e. a proposition of the form 'Something (e.g. happiness, virtue, pleasure, knowledge) is good'. Can any support be found for such a normative proposition? This is a notoriously controversial question in ethical theory which has been argued interminably. Some moral philosophers believe the problem can be solved by reducing propositions of value to propositions of some non-normative kind, through the device of defining the concept of goodness in terms of some non-normative concept. Given the definition of goodness, the normative proposition of value can now be reformulated in non-normative terms and supported by the kinds of arguments appropriate to the type of non-normative proposition to which it has been reduced.[3] But other moral philosophers would reject this line of argument, on the grounds that the concept 'good' is indefinable.

To pursue the merits of either side in this controversy here would be fruitless because it matters very little for our purposes whether 'good' can or cannot be defined. The crucial test of the axiological tradition lies elsewhere. The issue that must be resolved can be seen most clearly by turning to a form of utilitarianism in which the writer avoids the trap of attempting to derive our obligations from a recital of 'facts' by stipulating that 'goodness' is a unique concept, irreducible to any other. If such a utilitarian decides that it is his duty in a certain situation to do some specific act and is challenged to justify his decision, he can reply in very simple terms, by pointing out that the act he has chosen to do will produce more good than would be produced by any possible alternative act. If we put the utilitarian's reasoning into formal terms, however, we soon realize that the argument he has employed cannot support the conclusion he derives from it. Logically, his argument takes the following form: (1) A certain act that I can do will have such and such consequences, (2) These consequences are better than any I could produce by some other act I might do, therefore, (3) I ought to do this act. The inadequacy of the utilitarian's case results from the fact, which becomes obvious when we put his argument in formal terms, that it is logically invalid. For it has inserted in its conclusion a concept ('ought') that appears nowhere in its premises. To rescue their theory the utilitarians must plug this logical gap in their argument. The only way of doing so is to insert an 'ought' somewhere in its premises. This the utilitarians can do by pointing out that their theory itself, which stipulates that everyone ought always to maximize the good, operates as an implicit major premise in every argument they employ in reaching a decision about what act they ought to do in a concrete moral situation. If we add this premise to the two that I have given in the sample argument just above, we can overcome the formal objection to it. The logic of the utilitarians' argument is now impeccable; its conclusion follows without question from its premises.

But this formal validity has been bought with a price. For the purpose of their theory is to provide the utilitarians with a rational justification for the decisions they make about how they ought to act. To accomplish this goal they must appeal to an argument in which an essential premise is their own theory 'Everyone ought always to maximize the good'. Now the 'ought' in this premise is just as clearly a moral 'ought' as that in the conclusion 'I ought to do this act', which the premise is used to justify. So the same question can be raised concerning the premise that was raised earlier about the conclusion: How do the utilitarians justify the moral 'ought' that appears in their thesis 'Everyone ought always to maximize the good'? Obviously they believe the thesis to be true – it is their own theory – but what argument can they offer in its support? At this point the utilitarians are forced into a predicament from which they cannot be extricated. For any argument they may devise, if it is to support their thesis without committing a logical fallacy, must – as Prichard's dictum has made clear – include some premise that asserts a moral 'ought'. And then the original question, 'How do they justify the moral "ought"?' recurs. And on and on. In this way the utilitarians' attempt to provide an argument on behalf of their own theory and, by implication, in support of any practical decision they make about how they ought to act leads them inevitably into an infinite regress. For a utilitarian the question '*Why* ought we always to maximize the good?' is logically unanswerable. Yet the question is clearly reasonable, logically legitimate, and in certain kinds of concrete moral situation highly pertinent.

By his argument that an 'ought' cannot be derived from an 'is' Hume exposed the fatal weakness in a major tradition in Western ethical theory. However hard we try, we simply cannot reduce propositions that assert a moral obligation to, or deduce them from, propositions that state a 'fact'. But Prichard's dictum that an 'ought' can be derived only from another 'ought' cuts even more deeply into traditional ethics. For it lays bare the logical gap that separates propositions that assert obligations from those that assert values. Its revelation of a dualism within the realm of normative ethical propositions itself thus destroys the logic underlying the entire axiological tradition.

But if we cannot ground our beliefs about how we ought to act in an appeal to values, to what can we turn in their support? Prichard's contention, 'An "ought", if it is to be derived at all, can be derived only from another "ought",' although it cuts the ground from under traditional ethical theories, is not entirely negative. For it offers what may seem to be a viable alternative. Even though an 'ought' cannot logically be derived from anything else, at least it can be justified by an appeal to some other 'ought'. But will this really help us? An 'ought', if it is to function effectively in support of another 'ought', clearly must itself be justified. But the only way in which it can be justified is through an appeal to another 'ought' and, of course, this new 'ought' would also stand in need of justification. And so on. Instead of solving our problem the appeal to another 'ought' succeeds only in deferring it. Somewhere we must come to an 'ought' that we do not justify by an argument. Since all other methods of justification prove equally futile, we are forced to the conclusion that the logical objections that can be raised against any argument we might employ to support our beliefs about how we ought to act are insuperable. The attempt to justify our moral convictions by *argument* leads only to a dead end.

A number of moral philosophers (including Prichard) accept this conclusion with equanimity. Not only is it impossible for us to find arguments capable of justifying our moral convictions, they maintain, it is unnecessary as well. For we can know them to be true without recourse to argument. The attempt to *derive* an 'ought', even from another 'ought', is, thus, both a fruitless and a gratuitous undertaking. Such is the view of a final tradition in Western moral philosophy, which has come to be known as intuitionism. According to the intuitionists, we know that certain acts or types of acts are our duties because we directly 'apprehend' them to be so. Although intuitionists have given different accounts of the nature of our moral apprehensions – some speaking of our 'feelings' of obligation or referring to a 'moral sense' that everyone possesses and others, more rationalistically inclined, maintaining that we are capable of intuiting our duties by an act of 'intellectual insight' – all agree that the occurrence of a certain kind of experience in a human being, which they would characterize as 'the direct apprehension of duty', guarantees that the person ought to do the act so 'apprehended'. No argument can be given that will justify this moral apprehension but none is necessary. It is simply self-evident that we ought, for example, always to keep promises and never to tell lies. The moral 'ought' expressed in these injunctions is at once both non-derivative and self-justifying.

Can the intuitionists' thesis that the moral 'ought' needs no justification because it is self-justifying be sustained? To use a standard example of the intuitionists, do we know by self-evident insight that we have a duty to keep promises, as such? Although I have devoted much reflection to this question, I have not been able to convince myself of the self-evidence of such an obligation. Although I would readily admit that the duty to keep our promises is a very stringent one, I fail to find the obligation universal and unexceptional. It is not enough to say, as one intuitionist does, that the self-evidence of our duty to keep promises lies simply in the fact that 'a promise is a promise'. On the contrary, I think it possible to cite situations in which people have actually found themselves placed, in which a promise they have made, as far as I can discern, has no moral binding force on them *whatsoever*. And the same holds true of the duty not to tell lies or, I believe, any of the others that intuitionists cite.[4]

The intuitionists, of course, recognize that people will and do disagree about the duties they apprehend as self-evident. But such disagreement, they contend, proves only – what no one would deny – that we do not all possess equally acute insight into such matters. Indeed, the moral perceptiveness of some individuals is so blunt that intuitionists sometimes speak of them as being 'morally blind'. The trouble with such a solution to the problem of divergent intuitions is that it begs the question. It may well be true that the reason why I fail to intuit a duty to keep promises, as such, is simply that I lack the necessary acuteness of moral perception to apprehend it. But it may equally be true that the reason for my failure is that there is no such duty to apprehend and that, therefore, the intuitionists are 'intuiting' something that does not exist. And who is to decide which of us is correct, and how? The problem becomes even more serious when we discover that intuitionists not only disagree with non-intuitionists about the nature of self-evident moral truths but that they cannot even agree among themselves on the issue. For a study of the literature reveals cases in which one intuitionistic philosopher claims it to be self-evident that we have a certain duty and another claims it to be self-evident that we do not. Obviously one of the two must be mistaken. But how can we decide which one? To get over this difficulty intuitionists have sometimes made use of a distinction, between veridical intuitions and pseudo intuitions. Such a device does not solve the problem, however; it merely postpones it. For there is nothing in an intuition itself to mark it as pseudo or veridical. To the person who has the experience that he is directly apprehending an act to be his duty, his intuition must appear veridical. In order to authenticate an intuition as truly veridical, or to dismiss it as a mere pseudo intuition, the intuitionist must appeal to some criterion of truth capable of deciding the issue. Obviously he cannot appeal to any further intuition because the same question could be raised concerning it, making it necessary for him to establish its authenticity, so he would find himself trapped in an infinite regress. His remaining alternative – to evaluate the alleged intuition in terms of some criterion of truth other than intuitive self-evidence – is equally fatal to his case. For that is to admit that his justification for concluding that the intuition he has had is veridical lies not in the fact that he has had a direct apprehension of self-evident truth but rather that what he has affirmed to be true satisfies the alternative criterion to which he is now appealing. It is, in effect, to abandon intuitionism.

Finally, the intuitionistic view is faced with an insuperable logical difficulty. A veridical intuition of duty must be the apprehension by an individual of an objective fact – that a certain act is his duty.[5] One cannot have such an intuition unless the duty exists. Now, according to the intuitionists, people do have moral intuitions that are veridical. It follows, therefore, that in such situations the duties they intuit must exist. Let us suppose, then, that an intuitionist has a certain experience that he claims to be a veridical intuition of duty and someone challenges his claim, asking him to justify it. To do so he must demonstrate that the duty he claims to have intuited is real. But what evidence can he give for its existence? The *only* evidence he has is his experience, which he can describe, if he so desires, in the most minute detail. But no such description establishes the existence of the object alleged to have been experienced. Rather, to substantiate his claim that his intuition is veridical he must in his justification make a move from his experience to its object. The only way in which the intuitionist can do this is to argue that the existence of the experience somehow *guarantees* the existence of what is said to be experienced. Given the experience the reality of its object necessarily follows. Two objections, both fatal, can be raised against such an argument. On the one hand, it eliminates the possibility of pseudo intuitions. Whatever one 'intuits' to be his duty is his duty. It is impossible for anyone ever to make a moral mistake. But, more importantly, as an argument it simply breaks down. To be cogent it must establish a necessary link between two different things, an experience an individual has and a moral obligation he is alleged to have. That the two are different follows from the fact that the experience is, according to the theory, the apprehension *of* an obligation. The intuitionists must, therefore, demonstrate that it is impossible for a person to 'intuit' as his duty an act that he does not in fact have an obligation to do. To do so they must demonstrate that any statement of the form 'Person A "intuits" a duty to do act X but act X really is not his duty' is self-contradictory. But since the act of 'intuition' and the purported object of that act are different from each other no such demonstration is possible. Rather, the statement I have put in quotation marks is perfectly self-consistent.

Some intuitionists have toyed with the possibility of overcoming the logical weakness in their theory by eliminating the distinction between the experience of duty and duty itself. To have an experience that one is intuiting a certain moral obligation is to have the obligation because the two are the same. On reflection, however, most intuitionists have drawn back from this expedient, recognizing its disastrous implications.

For it leads logically to ethical nihilism. To say that our duties are identical with our experiences of duty is, in effect, to deny that we really do have any duties. All that remains is a certain peculiar kind of experience that people have. Although we may call this experience 'the intuition of duty', we must recognize that our language is misleading; for nothing remains to be intuited. The basis for a moral life is thus destroyed.

The conclusion to which this review of the major traditions in Western moral philosophy leads is that none has successfully answered the second of the two central questions of philosophical ethics: Why ought we to act in certain ways? Although my discussion has been brief, and hence far from exhaustive, I think it safe to say that a more thorough inquiry would serve only to reinforce the conclusion that the main attempts traditional ethicists have made to provide a satisfactory justification for any conclusions about how people ought to act have ended in failure. So what should one do? Many philosophers have seen no alternative but to become ethical sceptics. Although it would be an over-simplification of the situation to attribute the prevalence of ethical scepticism among contemporary philosophers to the kinds of problems I have raised (for many other factors have contributed to that result), nevertheless it remains true, in fact, that philosophers have been strongly influenced by such considerations and, in theory, that they ought to be so.

The philosophical implications that can be drawn from an acceptance of the dictum that an 'ought' can be derived only from another 'ought', thus, are very serious indeed. For it appears to lead inexorably to ethical scepticism – the conclusion that no theoretical justification can be found for any beliefs about how we ought to act. But the story does not end there. For theoretical conclusions can and do have practical consequences. In particular, the conclusion that no rational support can be given for a certain set of beliefs, if it becomes widely accepted, almost inevitably causes changes in practices associated with those beliefs. To take the obvious illustration: It is unquestionable that the general decline of belief in the tenets of Christian theology that has occurred in the past few centuries has brought in its wake a decline in the practice of the religious observances derived from those beliefs. If people become convinced that a set of beliefs is no longer rationally supportable, they will, perhaps slowly but almost surely, alter their behaviour accordingly. The generalization is particularly applicable to morality because the acts our moral convictions require of us are often acts that, given our natural inclinations, we would prefer not to do. To speak for myself, I think I can say in all honesty that, if I should become firmly convinced that no rational support could be found for any standard of moral conduct, this conviction would almost surely produce marked changes in my way of life. Nor do I consider myself peculiar in this; many other people, I believe, would respond in the same way. The practical result of ethical scepticism is, generally, moral cynicism.

But one thing must be made quite clear. The conclusion I have just reached should not be construed as an argument against ethical scepticism. Whatever its practical consequences, whether welcome or unwelcome, these are irrelevant to its truth or falsity. Whether I, or anyone else, accept or reject ethical scepticism should depend solely on the weight of argument that can be marshalled for or against it. My point here is only to emphasize that the issue with which I am concerned in this essay can have momentous practical consequences. And we should not blink this fact.

So much for the first three questions I raised at the beginning of this Part; I turn now, and for the remainder of the essay, to the last two: Can a theory be developed that is capable of meeting the objections that have so devastated traditional ethics and, if so, what should such a theory be? Let me begin by stating briefly the problem that faces us. Our objective is 'to justify the moral "ought"' – that is, to establish that we can give good reasons for affirming that some beliefs about how people ought to act are true. The central difficulty is to discover what kind of considerations can be offered in support of these moral beliefs. If the argument to this point is sound, we cannot derive a moral 'ought' from any set of premises (whether they be simply descriptive or even evaluative in nature) that do not already contain it, because any attempt to do so results in an argument that is logically fallacious. Although we can derive such an 'ought' from a set of premises that contain an 'ought', such a procedure is of no help, because it leaves us with a new 'ought' that requires justification and we are trapped in an infinite regress. Or we can, finally, argue that the moral 'ought' requires no justification because it is self-justifying, but such a move ends in intuitionism, against which unanswerable objections can be raised. If we approach the problem of moral justification in the terms of traditional ethics, these seem to be the only possibilities open to us. Since they all end in failure, we are left with only two further alternatives: Either we become ethical sceptics or we break with traditional ethics and find some new way of justifying morality. It is obvious that I intend to take the second alternative; otherwise I would not be writing this essay.

But what options remain open? The moral 'ought' is not self-justifying, it cannot be derived from a 'non-ought', and any attempt to derive it from another 'ought' leads to an infinite regress – unless some 'ought' can be found that *is* self-justifying. But what could such an 'ought' possibly be? Indeed, is it even meaningful to speak of a self-justifying 'ought'? To make the case I hope to defend, I must show that the concept of a self-justifying 'ought' is meaningful, that such an 'ought' does exist, and that a moral 'ought' can be derived from it. Before I begin my argument I think it would be wise to determine as clearly as we can just what the notion of 'ought' itself means. This is no easy job, for the concept is a very difficult and complex one, to which traditional writers – Kant is the great exception – have paid far too little attention.

NOTES TO PART I

[1] H. A. Prichard, 'Does Moral Philosophy Rest on a Mistake?' *Mind*, XXI (1912), 24. I should perhaps note that Prichard did not himself recognize fully the destructive implications of his statement:

I shall discuss this matter later in Part I. I might add also that other objections have been raised, especially in the twentieth century, against the possibility of our providing any justification for our moral beliefs. In particular, a view (which was quite widely accepted a generation ago) held that these beliefs had no cognitive significance because they were incapable of empirical verification. It has, however, been amply demonstrated that the grounds on which this view rested were untenable hence that they could not support the conclusions it reached about moral beliefs. Its challenge to moral knowledge, although it seemed serious at the time, has now faded away so need no longer be considered seriously.

[2] Since the crucial point lies in Prichard's main assertion, I shall concentrate on that, dropping the subordinate clause.

[3] The adoption of such a procedure implies, of course, an abandonment of the notion that the normative propositions of ethics are unique and a return, by implication, to some form of the view that we have already considered and found vulnerable to the critique of Hume.

[4] The intuitionist whom I just quoted regarding promises is W. D. Ross. Furthermore, the well-known distinction that he draws, between *prima facie* duties and actual duties, offers no answer to my argument, for I am contending that situations do occur in which people who have made a promise have no duty *whatsoever*, either *prima facie* or actual, to fulfil it. As for the duty not to tell lies, it requires little reflection to visualize situations in which one could with no moral qualms disregard it. And so on.

[5] I am using the term 'fact' here in the broad sense in which it means 'anything that is the case'.

II

WHAT does the term 'ought' mean? What information are we conveying to him when we tell a person that he ought to do a certain act? These are not easy questions to answer. For 'ought', like most other abstract concepts that we use regularly in our everyday discourse, does not wear its meaning on its face. We cannot offer a simple definition of it, as we might of a triangle or a tree. Perhaps the best way to start our examination of 'ought' is with an inquiry into the way in which it is ordinarily used. We must understand the role that the term plays in our conversation, to determine the functions it performs in our communications with, and our relationships to, each other. We must then go on and ask why it is used in the ways that it is. Our answer to this question, if it is to be adequate, will involve us in an inquiry into the nature of man's life, his modes of reasoning, and his social relationships. For it is in these basic facts of human existence that the concept has its origin and finds its meaning. If life and the world were sufficiently different from what they are, 'ought' as a moral concept would never have become a part of our vocabulary.

The first point that we must note about the term 'ought', as it is ordinarily used, is that it is not necessarily a moral concept. Rather, the term is employed in a wide variety of contexts, some of them non-moral and even anti-moral. For instance, people commonly say such things as 'You ought to see Naples before you die' or 'If you want to be successful in politics, you ought to give up your moral scruples'. Other examples could be cited, of different specific ways in which the word is used. What these illustrate is that 'ought' is a quite general concept in our vocabulary with a wide variety of applications, among which is its use as a distinctively moral concept.[1] Although it is conceivable that these various uses have nothing in common, the fact that they are uses of the same term provides strong *prima facie* evidence to the contrary. I shall start with the assumption, which I hope to confirm, that the various uses do have common characteristics, which justify our employing the same word even when the specific contexts of its use are quite different in many respects from each other. In order to understand the moral meaning of 'ought', which is our concern here, the best procedure probably is to look first at the term in a general way, attempting to pick out the characteristics that are common to it in whatever particular kind of context it is being used, and then go on to find the distinguishing marks that separate its moral usage from all the others. The explication of 'ought' in general, with which I shall begin, will take up several pages, so I want to make it clear now that my use of the term will for some time have no moral connotations. When it comes time to turn from the general to the specific, and begin to talk in moral terms, I shall mark the shift.

'Ought' is an odd concept. If I say to a travelling friend 'You ought to see Naples', I am not making a prediction about the itinerary he will follow because I realize that he may not take my advice. My statement thus is in a sense weaker than a descriptive statement, such as 'Since you are going south to visit Pompeii you will see Naples too'. In another sense, however, it is stronger. For in making it I lay my friend under a kind of constraint. To some degree I limit his freedom of action. If he listens at all to my advice, he cannot make his travel plans oblivious to what I have said. Yet the constraint does not amount to compulsion. I am not forcing him to visit Naples, for he may stop short at Rome. Rather, the force of an 'ought' statement seems to lie somewhere along the line that leads to outright compulsion at its extreme end. To understand the meaning of 'ought', we must clarify the nature and discover the grounds of its quasi-compulsive force. To do this will require a rather lengthy discussion.

As the example I have just used indicates, when we tell a person that he ought to perform a certain act, we do so, unless we are speaking idly, in the hope of evoking a response from him. If he heeds our words and agrees with what we say, he will do some act – or, because we often say that a person ought *not* to do something – refrain from doing an act that he might otherwise have done. 'Ought', thus, is concerned with human actions. But we must interpret the term 'action' broadly here, to cover a wide variety of responses, including such things as feelings, beliefs, and attitudes as well as overt physical acts. For we commonly tell a person, for example, that he ought to alter his feelings about someone else and hardly any admonition is more of a commonplace than 'You ought not to believe everything you hear'.

Why do people often, although by no means always, heed admonitions like these, especially when their doing so leads them to act in a way that thwarts their immediate and sometimes very strong inclinations? An illustration will furnish the best beginning to an answer to this question. Suppose I say to some friend, who is earning and spending a substantial income each year: 'You ought not to squander every cent you earn. You can get along on much less. The time may well come when you won't be earning any more and then you will welcome the money you have set aside. You ought to save for a rainy day.' My friend, if he cares about his own well-being and has enough imagination to look into the future, will probably recognize the wisdom in my words and, if he has the necessary willpower, will follow my advice and change his way of life. And if he were asked to justify his action he would probably reply simply that common prudence demanded it. But what if we should press him further, by asking him why he has decided that he ought to live prudently rather than improvidently? To any ordinary person the answer to such a question would be obvious. If one is interested in his own welfare, the reasonable thing for him to do is to make some provision for the future. To squander every cent he earns, even if he is strongly tempted to do so, would be the height of folly. Because it would be detrimental to his own long-range interests, such action would be irrational and indefensible, hence he ought not to do it.

The relationship between 'ought' and human actions, thus, is a special one, concerned with the reasons we have for doing what we do. To tell a person that he ought to do something is not to force him to do it, for he may ignore our advice, but it is to imply that we have good reasons for so advising him. If he does disregard what we have said, he is acting irrationally, for, if our advice is sound, he cannot give any satisfactory reasons for his response. Rather, to respond rationally he must act in the way that we have advised. But what if we are mistaken in what we say? What if it should turn out that he can give better reasons for doing some other act than the reasons we give for the act we say he ought to do? Then our 'ought' loses its force. To return to our illustration, the individual who is spending all his earnings may have a secret trust fund set aside in his name, so have no worry about rainy days.

The fact that our judgments about what people ought to do can be, and often are, mistaken makes it practically urgent for us to devise some way by which we can determine whether any particular decision a person makes is correct or not. The method we must use is clear from what has already been said. The cogency of any conclusion we reach about how anyone ought to act depends on the weight of argument we can marshall in its behalf. Sometimes people find it fairly easy to justify their decisions. In a situation involving a choice between a course of action that is prudentially wise and another that is sheer and obvious folly, few people would hesitate to agree both that they ought to pursue the first course and that this decision is rationally well-founded. As soon, however, as the situation facing us becomes complex, involving several possible alternative courses of action for which reasons of weight can be advanced, the decision about what we ought to do becomes a difficult and sometimes hazardous one to make. We cannot be sure that any decision we reach is correct; the best we can do, if we respond rationally, is to choose the alternative that we can back with the strongest reasons.

To sum up, 'ought', in its general usage, rests on and is justified by the reasons that we have for performing deliberate acts. The process of practical deliberation consists in weighing the arguments that can be advanced in support of each of the alternative courses of action open to us and deciding that the act for which the strongest reasons can be given is the act we ought to do. This analysis, nevertheless, leaves some questions remaining: How do we go about evaluating arguments, to determine which of several competing ones is the strongest? And, more specifically, is it ever possible to discover an argument in favour of a given act that is so conclusive that it rules all alternative acts out of consideration, permitting us to decide without question that that act alone is the act we ought to do? Since the second question is of vital importance to the issue of moral justification, we shall have to consider it with some care. Before turning to it, however, we should finish our examination into the meaning of 'ought' by considering the concept in which we are particularly interested in this essay – the moral 'ought'. What we have just said is general, applying to 'ought' in all of its various uses. We must now try to set out the differentia that distinguishes the specifically moral 'ought' from all others.

If someone tells me that I ought to do a certain act, I cannot conclude from the words he has used that he is offering me moral advice. For he may be implying that the act he is urging on me will promote my own interests and, hence, that I ought to do it for purely prudential reasons. But when people give advice that they consider to be moral almost always they are concerned about the effects that one's actions will have on others. The context into which the concept of moral obligation naturally fits and from which it derives its distinctive meaning is the social life of man and, in particular, the consequences of each individual's acts on the welfare of his fellows. To understand why this is true will require an examination into the nature of man and society.

I shall begin with a very basic question: Why does human life have a moral dimension? What is there about man's nature and existence that gives his actions moral significance? As far as we know, man is the only kind of living creature to whom morality is relevant. What sets him apart? Two characteristics, both of which we possess, are essential. On the one hand, we are, like other animals, creatures with wants and desires. Every day each of us has a myriad of desires, ranging from the merest flicker of interest in some passing object to a life-long quest for *happiness*. I have italicized the word 'happiness' because it will be a central concept in the theory that I shall advance in this essay. If one were asked to sum up men's desires in a single, general statement, the best response he could give would be to say 'All men desire to be happy'. The concept denoted by the English word 'happiness' is one of the most felicitous in our vocabulary. For what may appear to be a serious defect, its vagueness, is its greatest merit. The 'quest for happiness' provides a vast explanatory umbrella under which almost all of the objects of men's desires, no matter how varied they may be, can be gathered.[2]

The term 'happiness', as I am using it here, is a purely descriptive concept, having no normative connotations. It can be defined in terms of the relationship between a person's desires, whatever they may be, and their fulfilment. He is happiest whose desires are most completely fulfilled and least often frustrated; he is most unhappy whose desires are forever frustrated and never fulfilled. Such an interpretation allows no room for one to draw qualitative distinctions between various types of happiness, saying, for example, that a certain kind of happiness is 'higher' in nature than another. Nor do I believe that any such qualitative distinctions are supportable. I disagree, therefore, with Aristotle's normative categorization of happiness in the *Ethics*, in which the happiness of the philosophical life is held to be intrinsically superior to that of any other mode of human existence. I have several reasons for my disagreement. In the first place, Aristotle's account accomplishes nothing that cannot be done equally well with my interpretation. Presumably he believed it necessary to discover a 'higher' happiness in the life devoted to philosophy than in one devoted, say, to the pursuit of honour in order to give a rational justification for the life he lived and to encourage others to follow his example. But, should I wish to accomplish the same aim, I could do so by arguing that the philosopher is the happiest of men for the simple reason that he gets *more* happiness from life than anyone else. (I should add, parenthetically, that this is an argument I would be very reluctant to use. As a result I find myself hesitant about advising anyone to become a philosopher, at least for the happiness he will enjoy in such a life. Personally I have always felt that the happiest life would be that of the successful creative artist, particularly the composer; unfortunately, since I am quite lacking in musical talent, my pursuit of such a career would have been a constant exercise in frustration.)

In addition, Aristotle is faced with the problem of justifying his thesis that the happiness of the philosopher is 'higher' than that of anyone else. How does he know this to be true? In answer he provides a set of arguments based on his conception of the nature of man, which, unfortunately, turn out to beg the essential question. But is it possible in any way to defend the thesis that some types of happiness are 'higher' than others? This question leads to a final criticism of any view like that of Aristotle. For those who draw qualitative distinctions between different kinds of happiness must face a logical problem, that of specifying a criterion in terms of which they can make these distinctions. If one kind of happiness is 'higher' (as distinct from quantitatively greater) than another, it must contain some ingredient other than happiness itself to give it this superiority. For, if I say 'Person A is happier (i.e. enjoys greater happiness) than person B but B nevertheless is happier (i.e. enjoys a higher kind of happiness) than A' – as the Aristotelians must be prepared to do – I am clearly talking some kind of nonsense. For I have failed to make a vital distinction that alone will render my verdict about A and B meaningful. To say what I want to say, I must restate my comparison in some such way as 'Person A is happier (i.e. enjoys greater happiness) than person B but B nevertheless has a better life than A (i.e. his experience contains an ingredient – or ingredients – that A's does not, which more than compensates for the lesser happiness he enjoys).' If this is true, the advice that we should seek the 'highest' kind of happiness in life is misleading. Rather we should not simply seek happiness as such but the new ingredient, whatever it may be, which renders certain kinds of experience superior to others. For it is it, and not happiness, that must be considered the 'highest' quality of experience available to man.[3]

One important qualification: Although I do not accept the Aristotelian tradition with its distinction between 'higher' and 'lower' kinds of happiness, I do not go to the opposite Benthamite extreme of analysing the notion of happiness into the terms of a quantitative hedonism. Such an interpretation would be legitimate only if human desires were limited to the pursuit of pleasure. But this they most manifestly are not. The hedonistic view that men find their happiness exclusively in the enjoyment of pleasure, by reducing the rich diversity of our interests and activities to a single narrow pursuit, implies an impoverished conception of human nature that the facts of life, as we find them actually to be, simply do not support.

In his central thesis – that the most general goal of human life is happiness – Aristotle is certainly right. We all do seek happiness; unfortunately, however, we by no means all find it. It would be beside the point, as well as beyond my ability, to explain why we so often fail to find the happiness we are seeking in life. Yet it is possible to point out one major impediment, of crucial moral significance, that stands in the way of each individual's quest for happiness. This is other people. In their pursuit of happiness, individuals constantly run afoul of each other. Two people find themselves wanting the same object – a wife, a job, an office – which only one can have. In such a conflict of desires we have the paradigm of all practical moral problems. Although the complications of the basic situation are infinite, the conditions that generate the moral dimension of human life lie in the conflicting desires of different individuals, in which the satisfaction of one person's desire must be purchased by the frustration of another's.

Yet we do not create morality simply by having conflicting desires. Individual animals also have desires whose fulfilment thwarts those of other animals, but it does not follow that they are confronted with moral problems as a result. What distinguishes humans whose desires are in conflict from animals is the means they have available to them to resolve their problems. To decide such issues animals resort to force – the stronger bull moose often leaves his rival dead on the snow during mating season – or, at most, to cunning. Although men, too, employ the same methods, they are not limited to them. For they can, in addition, adjudicate their conflicts rationally. They can ask themselves: 'Which contestant ought to have his desire satisfied and which ought to give way?' and can then go on to answer their question by determining whose case can be supported by the stronger set of reasons. It is this distinctive ability that makes man a moral being and adds to human life its moral problems.

To sum up, two conditions give rise to the moral dimension of human life – the conflicts that result from the opposed desires of different individuals and man's capacity to resolve these conflicts by the use of reason. Both are essential to moral life but neither alone is sufficient.

The purpose of this discussion has been to explicate the meaning of 'ought', in its distinctively moral connotation. If we become involved in a practical conflict of interests and have to make a decision about what to do, we must ask ourselves whether the arguments we have to give in support of pursuing our own interests are as strong as those that the other person has to offer in his own behalf. If we find ourselves forced to answer this question in the negative, then we must conclude that, because we cannot justify doing anything else, we *ought* to give way, deferring our interests to those of the other person. The 'ought' in this judgment, because of the context in which it is used, is distinctively moral. It is our *duty* in this situation to defer to the other person. This interpretation of the distinctive meaning of the moral 'ought', based on an analysis of the kind of context in which it is appropriately used, assumes that it is possible for us to assess arguments given in support of different courses of action and reach sound decisions regarding their relative strength. In order to be able to do so, we must find some criterion in terms of which our assessments can be made and defended. Our next task, to which I shall turn in a moment, will be to establish such a criterion.

The connection between our use of 'ought', in a distinctive moral way, and our other uses of the term lies in the fact that in all cases the concept is concerned with the reasons we have to give in support of our actions. Its specific difference from these other uses results from the fact that the kind of actions to which it refers are those that, directly or indirectly, have consequences affecting the welfare of someone other than the agent. Both of these points might be made more clear by an illustration. Suppose I am doing a mathematical problem and, after much calculation, arrive at an answer. A friend, with a clearer head than mine, checks over my figures and remarks: 'Look, that answer won't do. You *ought* to have come out with ... instead.' To justify his comment he then takes me through my calculations and points out to me where I have committed an error. In admitting my mistake, I acknowledge his judgment. Because I cannot offer any argument to defend what I have done, I must agree with him that I ought to have done otherwise. Yet no question of morality has been raised. Although my friend has told me what I ought to do, the 'ought' he has used has no moral connotations; I have no *duty* to do mathematics according to the rules. Now suppose, however, that I am doing my mathematics as a bank cashier and that my miscalculations are part of a scheme I have worked out to defraud my employers. My act suddenly assumes a new significance; my obligation not to miscalculate, although it rests on the same grounds (namely, my inability to defend my results against mathematical criticism), is now moral. It is so because my acts have social consequences, with potential effects on the welfare of many people.

So much for the meaning of 'ought' in general and of the moral 'ought' in particular. We are now ready to turn directly to the substantive issues before us. The task we must accomplish is to find answers to the final two questions I raised at the beginning of the essay: Do objections like those posed by Prichard eliminate ethics as a legitimate philosophical discipline capable of providing a justification for moral beliefs or can an ethical theory be developed which succeeds in circumventing them and, if the latter, what must such a theory be? At the end of the first Part I suggested that the traditional moral philosophers, in their attempts to provide a theoretical justification for our beliefs about how we ought to act, had failed to consider one possible line of argument: To justify the moral 'ought' by deriving it from some 'ought' that is itself self-justifying. I shall now examine that possibility. My argument will proceed in four main steps, in which I shall attempt to answer the following questions: (1) What do I mean by a 'self-justifying "ought"'? (2) Is there any such 'ought' and, if so, what is it? (3) How can one derive a moral 'ought' from this self-justifying 'ought'? (4) What is the nature of the moral 'ought' so derived?

The first question can be answered quite briefly. The notion of 'ought', I have argued, must be understood in terms of the reasons we give for our actions (in the broad sense in which the term 'action' includes not only overt physical acts but such inner responses as beliefs and attitudes as well). In the various kinds of contexts in which such language is appropriate, when a person tells me that I ought to do something he is implying that I cannot give any good reasons for not doing it. The cogency of such an injunction, furthermore, is determined by the weight of the argument that can be marshalled in its support. To return to my mathematical illustration, my friend was correct in pointing out that I ought to have got a different answer than I did. I could not defend the answer I got because it violated the rules of mathematics. Nevertheless, a theoretical loophole does remain in this example. It is possible (in theory) that I was calculating in a system of mathematics different from his, in which the move I had made and, consequently, the answer I got did not involve an error. If I could show this to my friend, I would undermine his injunction, leaving him unable to justify his 'ought'. Now, by a self-justifying 'ought' I mean one that *cannot* be undermined by any argument. If I say to someone 'You ought to do this', my injunction is self-justifying only if I can demonstrate that it is theoretically impossible for him to give any reasons at all that could support his doing an alternative act. A self-justifying 'ought', thus, would be the same as an absolute 'ought'. Is there any such? That is our next question.

I shall begin by stating my case, then proceed to the argument by which I hope to justify it. There is at least one injunction that lays down an absolute, self-justifying obligation: 'One ought always to be rational.' Before I can defend this thesis I must make clear just what it means. The crucial term, of course, is 'rational'. What do we mean by rationality? Under what conditions do we say that a person is being rational or, alternatively, irrational? The answer is to be found in the reasons he has for the beliefs he accepts. Broadly speaking, a rational person is one whose beliefs are determined by the weight of evidence and argument that can be given in their support. In this sense, one may be rational even though he believes something that is in fact false, if he has better reasons for accepting it as true than he has for denying it as false. However, when new evidence or arguments are presented to him that shift the balance against his belief, the rational person will abandon it. The irrational person, on the other hand, clings to his beliefs regardless of the weight of either evidence or arguments.

Implied in the broad notion of rationality that I have just described lies a narrower conception of the term. The rational person, I have said, is the individual who bases his beliefs on the weight of evidence and argument in any given case. As this weight varies so will the strength of his conviction. If such a person discovers a proposition whose truth he can demonstrate, it follows that he will accept it without qualification. For the extreme of irrationality would be to deny a demonstrated truth, since that would mean the acceptance of a proposition as true for which it is logically impossible to offer any argument at all. When, therefore, I say that we have an obligation to be rational and that this obligation is self-justifying, the case I am presenting and hope to defend is that the obligation to accept as true a proposition whose truth has been demonstrated is absolute. But even if this were correct, would it have any relevance to the main issue with which I am concerned in this essay? To answer this question affirmatively, I must show that there are propositions which have implications for the moral life of man that satisfy the conditions I have just stated. It is my conviction that the thesis that one ought always to be rational is itself such a proposition. In the first place, it lays down an obligation that is absolute. And, although this obligation is not in itself moral (but rather rational), a moral obligation can be derived from it. I shall now try to support both these claims directly.

The thesis that we ought always to be rational may seem to some to be far from self-evident. One is prompted to ask 'Why?' The question is a perfectly natural one. But is it legitimate? That we must now try to see. Since my case for the reality of moral obligation rests on the narrow rather than the broad sense of rationality, I shall begin my argument by attempting to establish that the obligation we have to be rational, in this sense, is absolute. In what follows, therefore, the proposition 'One ought always to be rational' will be taken to mean 'One ought always to accept as true a proposition whose truth has been demonstrated'. (It might be noted that the obligation to be rational in the broad sense rests on the obligation to be rational in the narrow sense; for, if the latter obligation could not be sustained, the former would collapse as well.) The person who questions the position I am holding is committed, therefore, to the view that the obligation to accept as true a proposition whose truth has been demonstrated is not absolute. One can, in other words, legitimately reject such an obligation. My use of the term 'legitimate' here is important. For we are not concerned with the *possibility* of irrational belief. No one can deny that people *can* be irrational because in fact they often are.

The issue rather is whether they can defend their irrationality, whether they can present any arguments on its behalf.

Let us begin by looking at the case for the opposition. One who denies that the obligation to be rational is absolute must show that situations exist in which we can legitimately disregard it. To do so he must defend the following thesis: It is legitimate to accept as true a proposition the truth of whose denial has been demonstrated. Since a demonstrable truth is one whose denial is either self-contradictory or implies a contradiction, anyone assuming the view under examination is compelled logically to maintain the legitimacy of accepting as true a proposition that is either itself self-contradictory or implies a contradiction. If his acceptance of the truth of such a proposition is to be judged legitimate, he must be able to show it to be defensible. That is, he must produce some reason that justifies him in accepting the proposition as true. But this he cannot do. For if we accept the truth of his proposition we can demonstrate logically that we must accept the truth of its denial as well, because a proposition that implies a contradiction implies the truth of any other proposition, including its own denial. If we must accept the truth of its denial, however, we cannot accept its truth because the two are logically incompatible. Furthermore, since such a proposition implies its own denial, any reason that we might offer in its support would operate as a reason for accepting its denial. Therefore it could not function as a reason for affirming the truth of the proposition in question. Because it is logically impossible for us to offer any reasons for accepting as true a proposition that is self-contradictory or implies a contradiction, we cannot legitimately do so. On the contrary, all reasons lead logically to the affirmation of its denial. It follows that the injunction that we ought always to be rational – that we ought always to accept as true a proposition whose truth has been demonstrated – is absolute. Because the denial of this 'ought' leads to a contradiction, the 'ought' must be admitted to be self-justifying.

We seem thus to have answered our second question, by discovering an 'ought' that justifies itself. Before we can accept this step in the argument as having been accomplished, however, I think we must meet some objections. For example, someone might accuse me of having established my case by definition. My aim has been to provide an instance of a self-justifying 'ought'. What I have shown, however, is only that it is logically impossible for anyone legitimately to dispute the truth of a demonstrable proposition. On the basis of this conclusion I have argued that we all ought to accept such propositions as true because I have defined the concept of 'ought' in terms of the reasons we can give for the beliefs we hold. In other words, I have gained my objective not by my argument but by the way I have initially defined my crucial term.

My answer to this objection is twofold. First, I think my analysis of the meaning of 'ought' accurately reflects standard usage. 'Ought', as it functions in our ordinary discourse, rests on the reasons that people have for their actions (including their beliefs) in the way in which I suggested earlier in this Part. It would be perfectly normal for someone to tell another person 'You ought to abandon your position on this issue', if he had shown that the position was untenable on logical grounds. My analysis of the meaning of 'ought' is not a distortion developed to establish a case but an explication of what lies behind and supports our accepted employment of the term. Further, my case does not really depend on a definition of terms. Although I believe that I am using the concept 'ought' correctly, my primary concern is to establish that it is impossible for anyone to give any reasons that will justify him in accepting as true a proposition whose denial is demonstrable. Even though a person can, in fact, embrace such a proposition, he cannot legitimately do so. His action is illegitimate because it is rationally indefensible.

But this conclusion could lead to a further objection. For someone might accuse me of begging the question, by assuming the entire conclusion to be established; namely, that we ought never to believe anything that we cannot defend by argument. What answer, he might ask, can I give to the person who retorts,

'Granting everything you have said, I still want to know, Why ought I to be rational?' This question is clearly an attempt to undermine my whole position, for the person who asks it is refusing to accept the answer that I have already given as being really an answer to the question at issue. To meet the objection we must begin by asking just what anyone could mean by such a question. One possibility is apparent – that he is asking that I provide a *moral* justification for rationality. That is, when he asks 'Why *ought* I to be rational?' he is implying that he wants me to show him that it is his moral duty to be rational. And this, of course, I have not done. Nor have I tried to do it. The obligation to be rational, which I have contended to be self-justifying, is not in itself a moral obligation; whether a moral obligation can be derived from it is an issue we have yet to face. At this point I am content if I have succeeded in establishing a self-justifying rational obligation and that I think I have done.

The objector, however, would probably have another point lying behind his question. For he might well admit that I have shown irrationality to be logically indefensible but simply shrug his shoulders and say 'So what?' To such an irrationalist I would have a double response. First, I cannot prevent him from being irrational, nor am I interested (for the purpose of this argument) in doing so. The point at issue is not whether one can *be* irrational but whether one can *defend* his irrationality. And if he should ask 'Why do I need to defend my irrationality if I don't choose to do so?' I would reply that the issue with which we are concerned is one of truth. I have taken a position, which I claim to be true and which I have defended by arguments. Now it is quite irrelevant to the truth of my position that some person should decide that he will go on his own merry irrational way. In doing so he bothers neither me nor my theory, for I can simply ignore him. To raise an objection that can possibly compromise the truth of my conclusion he must be able to bring forward some argument in support of a view that contradicts it, in this case, the theory that irrationality is defensible. And that, as I have already shown, he cannot do.

We are now ready to turn to our third question: How can we derive a moral 'ought' from the self-justifying rational 'ought' we have just established? This question, besides being the most important one for the theory I am proposing in the essay, is also the most difficult to answer. To do so will require a long argument and will involve us in finding an answer to our final question as well: 'What is this moral "ought"'? So I shall take up both questions together.

The injunction that we ought always to be rational, although it is absolute, has no moral content. Because this is true our argument has not yet succeeded in producing a *moral* 'ought' that is self-justifying. What it has done, however, is to specify a condition that any such 'ought' must satisfy. Therefore what we must attempt to do is to find an 'ought' that satisfies this condition and at the same time expresses an injunction that is unquestionably moral. We must, in other words, transfer the kind of considerations I have just presented from the realm of beliefs to that of overt social actions. If we are successful we shall have derived a moral 'ought' from a self-justifying 'ought' by establishing that a single obligation satisfies the conditions both (1) of being logically inescapable and (2) of demanding action that is moral in nature.

Human life, I have argued, takes on a moral dimension when our acts affect the happiness of people other than ourselves, whether directly or indirectly. Furthermore, to determine what we ought morally to do we must consider the reasons we have to give in support of our proposed acts. If we can defend our performance of a certain act, then we are morally at liberty to do it; however, if we cannot defend it, we ought not to do it. The relevance of the argument we have just concluded to the problem of moral action, thus, should be quite apparent. For our rational obligations and our moral obligations both rest on the same grounds – the reasons we have to give in support of our actions, whether these be simply beliefs or overt acts with social consequences. If we cannot give any reason for believing a proposition to be true, we ought not to accept it; and if it can be shown that any reason we give for believing it is equally a reason for believing its denial, then our rational obligation to reject it becomes absolute. Likewise with our moral obligations. If we cannot give any reason for performing a certain act having social consequences, then we ought not to do it; and if any reason we give for performing it is equally a reason for not doing so – or for performing an alternative, incompatible act instead – then our moral obligation not to do that act is also absolute. For in both cases to do otherwise would be irrational.

Since my argument is now moving from the broad realm of actions that includes beliefs to the narrow realm in which it refers to overt physical acts, I shall introduce a new term, *arbitrary*, which can be applied to certain acts, in this narrower sense, in the same manner that *irrational* is normally applied to certain beliefs. As I shall be using this term, then, an act can be called arbitrary if it affects the happiness of persons other than the agent, either directly or indirectly, and is performed for a reason that is equally a reason for not performing it or, equivalently, for performing some alternative, incompatible act instead. Just as one ought not to embrace irrational beliefs (i.e. accept as true propositions for which no reasons can be given) so one ought not to perform arbitrary actions (i.e. do things that affect others for which no reasons can be given).[4] The injunction 'One ought not to be irrational' is absolute but has no moral content; but the injunction 'One ought not to act arbitrarily', besides being absolute, has moral content as well.

As it stands, however, it is practically impotent. If I tell a person that he has a duty never to act arbitrarily, I am laying down a moral injunction that he must accept. But I am not, by that fact, morally prohibiting him from doing any specific act. In order to accomplish this end and thus to make the injunction 'One ought never to act arbitrarily' relevant to man's moral life, I must establish that the notion of an arbitrary action has a practical application to everyday human affairs. I must, that is, identify certain acts that people in the normal course of events might perform and show that they are, according to my definition of the term, arbitrary. Rather than attacking this point directly, I shall approach it obliquely, by returning to look further at the notion of happiness.

Earlier in this Part, I said several things about happiness: That the concept is felicitously vague, that we may conceive of happiness as the general object of human desires, that people find their happiness in widely divergent pursuits and activities, and that one cannot make qualitative, but only quantitative, distinctions between types of happiness. I should like here to make a few more comments on the subject of happiness. Although I have spoken of happiness in terms of the maximum satisfaction of our desires, I have not attempted to describe it in its essence or immediacy. This, I think, is far from easy to do. For one thing, I doubt very much that everyone experiences happiness in the same way and, going further, I am inclined to think that many of us can be happy without 'experiencing' happiness at all. I, certainly, would find it very difficult to answer with any assurance if someone were to ask me 'Are you happy now?' I could not introspectively examine my conscious experience, isolate an element in it that I would recognize as happiness, and then, on discovering its presence, reply 'Yes, I am happy'. Yet I am quite sure that I have been relatively happy at some times in my life and less happy at others – and even, on occasion, positively unhappy. And, on recollection, I can pick out the periods that have been the happiest ones for me. Naturally these have been associated with certain events that have occurred in my life; I can say – with reasonable accuracy, I believe – what has caused my happiness. But I find it much harder to say exactly in what my happiness itself has consisted. Was it a feeling? A state of mind? An attitude? Of this I am convinced, that it was not simply the feeling of pleasure. The hedonistic identification is, if my own experience is any criterion, an over-simplification that comes close to being a parody of happiness.

For one cannot enjoy momentary happiness or unhappiness as he can pleasure or pain; to be happy is to experience a kind of conscious life that extends over a considerable period of time and which may be interspersed with many sensations of both pleasure and pain. If I had to give a description of happiness, relying on my personal experience, the best I could do would be to say that it is a general quality or tone of our on-going conscious life which, although it may not be noticeable at the time, emerges fairly clearly in retrospect – especially after the passage of several years. Aristotle, of all the moral philosophers, seems to have appreciated best the elusive quality of happiness. For the very fact that *eudaimonia* is so extraordinarily difficult to translate indicates his awareness that no simple-minded analysis of the concept could do justice to such a complex characteristic of human life and experience.

Nevertheless, happiness has one characteristic that can be asserted without question. It is a personal, individual possession. If I am happy, the happiness is mine alone. And the same holds for every other individual. It is true that we speak of people 'sharing each other's happiness' or of someone 'finding his happiness in the happiness of others'. Although such expressions make perfectly good sense, properly understood, they cannot be taken to imply that happiness is a possession that can *literally* be shared by different people. Two people can be happy together but it is each one who is individually happy and the happiness of one may be greater or less than that of the other. For a person cannot possess the happiness of another individual, any more than he can possess his feelings or sense perceptions. All, in their essence as attributes of conscious life, must belong to each individual, alone.

I should now like to return briefly to my earlier contention that it is impossible to make qualitative distinctions within happiness, saying that one kind of happiness is 'higher' than another, but that happiness must be evaluated in quantitative terms alone. If this is correct it would be possible theoretically – although, of course, not practically – to calculate the total happiness in the world at any given time, the possibility of such a calculation being insured by the fact that the components making up the total are all qualitatively on a par with each other, hence in theory subject to mathematical computation. In any such calculation, furthermore, the question of what individual persons possessed this happiness would be irrelevant to the result. The same total amount of happiness could be distributed in an infinite variety of ways among the individuals who possessed it. From this it follows that, if an individual performs an act which produces a certain amount of happiness, the amount of happiness produced depends in no way on the individual identity of the persons who enjoy it. If we were asked to determine how much happiness was produced by the act, the question '*Whom*[5] did the act make happy?' would be quite irrelevant to our inquiry.

Using these conclusions, we can now pose a hypothetical moral problem. Suppose a person is confronted with a decision between performing one of several alternative acts. He has convinced himself that by doing any one of these acts he can produce a considerable amount of happiness, and that the amount of this happiness will be the same no matter which alternative he chooses. The only difference between the alternatives is that if he performs act A person X will be made happy, if he performs act B person Y will be made happy, and if he performs act C person Z will be made happy. What ought he to do? The man's dilemma is clear. Under the conditions we have stipulated, whichever alternative he should choose, he would be acting arbitrarily. For his action will have social consequences yet, if he were to try to justify his performing any one of the alternative acts, the reason he would have to give would be an equally good reason for his performing another of the alternatives instead, hence could not function as a reason in favour of his performing the alternative he has chosen. We are forced to conclude, therefore, that under these circumstances (i.e. assuming that he had no other reasons on which to base a choice) the person ought to refrain from action. For to do otherwise would be to act arbitrarily.

The results to which my argument so far leads can be summed up in the form of a rule of moral action. This rule, which I shall call the Principle of Personal Impartiality, can be stated as follows: One ought never to do any act having social consequences that discriminates between persons on the basis of their individual uniqueness alone. Three small points of clarification might be helpful here. When I speak of an act that has 'social consequences' I mean an act whose results either directly or indirectly affect the happiness of someone other than the agent. And when I speak of 'individual uniqueness' I refer to the fact that every person, as such, is a unique human being, distinguishable from every other. Finally, in the phrase 'discriminates between persons' the persons in question include not only other people but the agent himself as well. The argument behind the Principle could be put in the following way: Because individual uniqueness is a characteristic that every person possesses equally, it cannot be used as a reason for discriminating in favour of (or against) any one person rather than any other. Such discrimination is, therefore, necessarily arbitrary (in the technical sense I have given to the term) and for that reason immoral.

What I have attempted to do in the Principle of Personal Impartiality is to find a way in which the moral injunction against arbitrary action that I laid down a bit earlier in this Part can be applied to the concrete decisions we must make in our everyday lives. My purpose in this has been to give some positive, practical content to that injunction. How well have I succeeded in my aim? One might argue that I have not moved my case appreciably forward because the Principle of Personal Impartiality does not in fact provide us with a moral injunction capable of helping us to make concrete decisions in our practical affairs. That this is so is indicated by the artificiality of the hypothetical moral situation which I posed in the illustration with which I introduced the Principle. Real human beings never – or, at least, seldom – find themselves in a situation in which their *only* ground for selecting between the possible recipients of their favours is the individual uniqueness of the persons concerned. For they always can find other reasons for discrimination.

Let us examine this issue further. First, a preliminary point. We must distinguish between the reasons we actually have for performing a certain act and the reasons we might have for performing that same act. It is quite true that we can generally (after the fact) discover reasons for having done some act in which we have discriminated between persons that will show that we have not acted arbitrarily at all. The mere fact, however, that we not only know what the term 'rationalization' means but also recognize its moral connotations rules out the legitimacy of such *ex post facto* explanations. So the question that we must face is: Do people often, or ever, act in a way that discriminates between individuals and have, as their only reason for this discrimination at the time that they act, the fact that the person favoured is the unique individual he is?

Once we understand what this question means I think we are forced to answer it in the affirmative. Indeed, I would go so far as to say that in a large proportion of our acts all of us discriminate in favour of some person on the basis of his individual uniqueness alone – ourselves. That this is true becomes apparent when we consider the motivations that lie behind much of what we do. The reason that we would normally have to give, if we were asked why we did a certain act, would be that we wanted to do it. And to say that we do an act because we want to do it is to imply, in most instances, that we do it in order to gain some end that we desire.[6] Finally, although the consideration may not always enter consciously into our minds, our performance of the act is an episode in our quest for happiness. When we act in this way the very nature of our motivation prevents us from weighing the welfare of others against our own and making a deliberate decision about what to do. We simply pursue our own interests because they are ours and we desire to realize them – without any thought for anyone else. Whenever we act in such a way (and how often do we all do so?) we are discriminating in favour of ourselves, for no other reason than that we are ourselves.

But is such action arbitrary and therefore immoral? It is, according to the definition I have given of arbitrary action, only if what we do has social consequences. And to seek one's own happiness, it may be argued, need not affect the happiness of anyone else. It is here that the qualifying phrase 'directly or indirectly' that I give in my explanation of the Principle of

Personal Impartiality becomes important. To pursue one's own ends may not always directly affect the welfare of others; however, it almost surely will affect that welfare indirectly. When we are motivated in acting simply by a desire for our own happiness, we fail, in that act, to take into consideration the happiness of anyone else. Had we done so, we might well have performed some other act instead. Thus we purchase our own happiness, at least indirectly, at the expense of that of others. The pursuit of personal happiness, to which we all devote so much energy, cannot justify itself, unless reasons can be given showing that our pursuit is consonant with that of our fellows. By addressing itself to this necessity the Principle of Personal Impartiality not only makes itself relevant to the concrete moral decisions of everyday life but applies to most of the acts we perform.[7] To do anything, especially if our act will have significant consequences, *simply* because we want to do it, and without consideration of its effects on others, is to act arbitrarily and hence immorally. For it is to discriminate against the happiness of others in favour of our own just because it is *our* happiness. No matter how much we may want to do a certain act, all of us have a duty before we act to ask ourselves if we can rationally justify what we are about to do, and then to act accordingly. The realm of moral action, in other words, is coextensive with that of significant practical action.

My conclusion – that it is wrong to pursue one's own interests just because they are one's own and without consideration of the interests of others – is a view that many people, including some moral philosophers, would not accept. Rather than attempting to survey all the opposed theories here, I shall limit myself to an examination of the view that stands at the opposite extreme to my own. This is ethical egoism, which has had occasional defenders throughout the history of philosophy, but is, perhaps, more important practically as the working philosophy of life of a good many people. In criticizing it I shall endeavour to show that its weaknesses can be overcome only by accepting the conclusions I have reached. The disagreement between the two theories can be put as follows:

Whereas the egoist holds that each individual person has an obligation to seek only his own happiness, without any regard to that of anyone else, I hold that, in promoting happiness, each of us ought to take into consideration the happiness of all individuals equally and that, therefore, we cannot morally justify ourselves in seeking our own happiness at the expense of that of anyone else, simply because it is our own.

Historically, egoists have given a variety of arguments in support of their view. One – which was particularly popular among certain eighteenth-century writers – is the thesis that self-interested action is in fact socially beneficial. According to the theory, if every individual in a society were assiduously to cultivate his own interests exclusively, the ultimate consequence would be the greatest happiness of the society in general. In Mandeville's neatly ambiguous phrase 'Private vices, public benefits'. How much truth there is in this generalization would be hard to determine, although the results of its practice in *laissez faire* economics would seem to cast considerable doubt on its cogency. In any event, we do not need to answer that question here because the argument itself involves an abandonment of the egoistic theory. The case the egoist must defend is that each individual ought to pursue his own happiness exclusively simply because it is *his own* happiness; to justify the pursuit of self-interest on the grounds that such action conduces best to social welfare is to imply, on the contrary, that we do have obligations to others. It is to shift from an egoism of ends to an egoism of means. And, although it may be an implausible doctrine of means, it need not be inconsistent with the conclusions I have reached.

If we put aside all arguments in favour of egoism based on the supposed socially felicitous consequences of self-regarding action, the only way that remains to defend the theory seems to be in discovering something special in the fact that the happiness he promotes by his acts will be his own, which can justify an individual in pursuing that happiness without regard to the happiness of anyone else. Certainly no analysis of the experience of happiness itself, as an actual ingredient of human life, will support the egoists' case. For the desirability of happiness does not depend on the individual who experiences it. One might get around this conclusion by arguing that one's own happiness is qualitatively superior to that of anyone else, except that I have already given reasons for rejecting the belief that different experiences of happiness can be distinguished from each other on qualitative grounds. But even if the contrary were true, it would not help the egoists. For their argument would then have to take the form that each person ought to seek his own happiness exclusively because this happiness is qualitatively superior to the happiness of everyone else. But that is impossible; there cannot be innumerable experiences of happiness, each of which is qualitatively superior to all the others.

But we have not yet got to the heart of the egoists' case. What they contend is that each individual ought to promote his own happiness exclusively because it is *his own*. The crucial concept is 'his own happiness'. What does this description mean as it figures in the egoists' theory? We can agree immediately that the phrase implies that happiness is a personal possession; each individual enjoys *his own* happiness but cannot experience that of anyone else. But this interpretation won't do the egoists' job. Since the happiness of *every* individual is a personal possession, to base a theory of obligation on this fact would be to imply that each of us ought to promote the happiness of all, without any regard to persons. One further possible interpretation remains to be investigated – that the phrase 'his own happiness' implies that the happiness in question is enjoyed by the person who by his own actions produces it. According to the egoists, each individual ought to seek his own happiness (and no other) simply because he will himself enjoy it. So the egoists must discover something peculiar in an experience of happiness that is self-produced, which does not occur in such an experience produced by the actions of another, that can justify an individual in concentrating his energies on promoting this kind of experience exclusively. Two lines of argument seem possible. It could be maintained, first, that each person ought to seek his own happiness exclusively, because, if his activities are successful, he will himself enjoy the happiness that results. In other words, the obligation to act rests on the fact that the resulting happiness will be self-enjoyed. But then, if any given individual ought to pursue his own happiness on the grounds that he will himself enjoy it, every other individual ought to pursue the same happiness (i.e. that of the first individual) for the same reason. For whether I produce my happiness myself or you produce it, I will equally enjoy it myself (it will be 'my own happiness'). And the reverse holds true for your happiness. Whether you produce it or I produce it, you will still enjoy it yourself. Hence each of us, on these grounds, finds himself with an obligation to promote the happiness of others that is equal to and indiscriminable from his obligation to promote his own. But this is a direct denial of the egoistic theory in favour of its exact opposite, the theory which I have been putting forward in this Part.

Here, however, an egoist might object, arguing that my interpretation of 'his own happiness' misses the vital point of his argument. For he does not mean by 'self-enjoyed' happiness what I have, in my criticism, taken him to mean. Rather he means that the happiness in question is enjoyed by the *same* individual who by his action produces it. On this interpretation his argument takes the following form: Every person ought to promote his own happiness exclusively because the result will be a 'happiness he has himself produced'. If 'his own happiness' is understood in this way, it is clear that no one can enjoy it except the agent who produces it. But let us look at this argument more closely. Its purpose is to justify a person's performing a certain act. The egoist argues: I ought to perform act A because, if I perform it, my doing so will produce happiness for me. Just what is it in this argument (understood in terms of the stage we have now reached in our discussion) that can justify the egoist in performing act A? Whatever it is must lie in some feature of the situation described as 'happiness he has himself produced'. Now it cannot be the happiness he will personally gain as a result of doing the act because we have already eliminated that by our earlier argument, so it must be the self-production of this happiness. In other words, the only feature that remains (as far as the egoist's argument is concerned) to set act A apart, and, by doing so, provide a reason to justify him in performing it, is the fact that he performs it himself. So the egoist is reduced to the argument: I ought to do act A because, if I do it, I will be doing act A. But as an argument this leaves a good bit to be desired.

I have chosen to comment on the position of extreme ethical egoism – that one has moral obligations only to himself – because it offers the sharpest contrast to the theory I am developing in this essay. But it should be noted that similar criticisms can be made of moderate egoism, or the view that each individual has a greater obligation to promote his own happiness, simply because it is his own, than to promote the happiness of anyone else. In both cases, such discrimination in favour of oneself proves to be arbitrary, hence incapable of moral justification. Furthermore, my criticisms apply not just to arbitrary self-interested action but equally to action in which we arbitrarily discriminate between individuals other than ourselves. Although this type of discrimination may not be so prevalent as self-interested action, nevertheless it occurs regularly. Whenever we act in a way that favours a certain individual at the expense of others for no reason except that we want to favour him we are acting arbitrarily. If we do discriminate between individuals, we must have some other reason to justify ourselves than the bare fact that we want to do so. Since almost every practical decision (beyond the most trivial) that we make is potentially discriminatory, morality demands that we deliberate before we act. To live a human life is to live a moral life, whether we do it well or ill. There is no practical escape.

I should like to conclude this Part by raising two objections to the view I have developed in it and by noting one implication of that view. The first of the objections can be dealt with briefly but the second, as well as the implication, will require lengthy discussion and will have to be carried over into Part III.

The first criticism, which concerns the Principle of Personal Impartiality, can be put as follows: The Principle fails to provide any basis for a *positive* obligation to our fellow-men. For one could satisfy its requirement of strict impartiality by a policy of moral neutralism, that is, by doing nothing to promote the happiness of anyone. But even further, the Principle seems to countenance a policy of anti-morality. For nothing is, in the eyes of most people, more heinous than disinterested cruelty, yet, because it is strictly impartial in its victims, it seems to have the full blessing of the Principle.

To rescue the Principle from this criticism, which would be disastrous to the theory I am developing, we must show that it lays us under an obligation to act not just impartially but positively to further the interests of our fellows equally with our own. The solution to the problem is quite simple; the clue to it lies in the last phrase of the previous sentence. If we had no desires of our own or if, even, we never performed any act to satisfy those desires, then it might plausibly be claimed that we had no obligation, in terms of the Principle, to further the interests of anyone else. Moral neutralism, as far as the question of impartiality is concerned, is consistent with total personal apathy – but with nothing more. And none of us is completely apathetic; far from it.[8] Rather we are all creatures of desire and we all act to satisfy our desires. As long as human nature remains in these vital respects as it is, we have, according to the Principle of Personal Impartiality, an obligation not only to treat everyone impartially but positively to promote the happiness of others to the same extent that we promote our own.

Next, to the implication of my theory. I want not only to emphasize that the stand I have taken to this point is morally extreme but to show, by brief illustration, just how extreme it is. According to the Principle of Personal Impartiality each of us has an obligation to promote equally the happiness of all, with no respect to persons. This duty must be taken literally. If the welfare of a human being will be affected by what I do, then, no matter who that person may be, I have an obligation to him that is equal, in principle, to my obligation to any other individual. I owe as much morally to an inhabitant of the interior of China as I do to my next-door neighbour. And the same holds true in the reverse direction. The effects of what we do, furthermore, are not limited to the present; rather our acts can have consequences that stretch far into the future. For example, although I have as yet no grandchildren, I have several rapidly-growing children. The way in which I rear these children will almost surely have indirect consequences in the lives of their as-yet-unborn children. Or, if I consider my moral responsibilities as a teacher, I must recognize that my influence on my students can have consequences not only in their own lives but in the lives of their children or of students they may someday themselves be teaching. And so on. Nor do I consider my obligations in any way unusual; although the details may vary from person to person, the general pattern is the same. All of us have obligations that stretch into the future, beyond our own lives into those of generations not yet born. If one considers his appearance on the human scene from a moral point of view, the irrelevancy of his space-time location becomes apparent. It is morally indifferent that I should be living in America in the mid-twentieth century; I might just as well be living somewhere else at some other time.

It is clear from what I have just said that none of us can completely fulfil his moral obligations, as those are laid down in the Principle of Personal Impartiality. We all fall short of moral perfection, hence all are morally culpable. How great, then, is our culpability? And is there any way (other than renewed moral effort) by which we can mitigate it? Not only are these reasonable theoretical questions to raise but they are, in addition, issues of practical concern for anyone who takes the moral life and its demands seriously. I shall return to them later as I elaborate my theory fully but first I wish to consider the second objection to the theory as it now stands.

By specifying the conditions under which an action would be arbitrary, the Principle of Personal Impartiality attempts to provide us with a criterion we can use in deciding what we ought and ought not to do. If an act violates the Principle, it is immoral; if it does not, it is morally acceptable. But is the criterion set up by the Principle to distinguish the moral from the immoral fully satisfactory? Can we always use it to determine what we should and should not do? Even if we grant that we often act in a way that discriminates between people with no more reason for doing so than our interest in the welfare of some individual person (whether ourselves or someone else)—and hence, according to the Principle, act immorally – such an explanation by no means accounts for all the considerations that move us to act. On the contrary, we often have reasons for making the decisions we do that appear to be quite different, reasons, furthermore, that seem to satisfy the conditions of morality laid down by the Principle. For example, I may act in a way that discriminates in favour of a certain person and, asked to justify myself, might honestly reply 'He's my brother'. Now this explanation – or any one of an innumerable list of possible alternatives – does not violate the injunction laid down in the Principle. For I have not discriminated simply on the basis of the personal uniqueness of the individual I have favoured. My reason for favouring him has in fact been quite different. Are such discriminatory acts, then, all morally acceptable? A person with no theory to defend might well reply in the affirmative. So let us alter the illustration slightly. Suppose I discriminated *against* an individual and, when asked to justify myself, replied 'He's my brother'. What would the ordinary person's response then be? And why? Or, to explore the problem in a different direction, suppose I gave as my reason for discriminating in favour of (or against) an individual 'He's red-headed' or 'He's the first person I met after I saw a falling star'. Speaking again for the ordinary person I can well imagine his rejecting such reasons on the grounds that they are morally irrelevant to my action. Yet they seem to be, as far as the Principle is concerned, quite legitimate reasons for discrimination.

The purpose of these illustrations is to raise questions concerning the adequacy of the Principle of Personal Impartiality by arguing that the criterion it establishes for distinguishing between acts that are morally acceptable and those that are not has loopholes in it. Its net is too coarse. Although it lays down an injunction against some of our acts, it has nothing to say about others. To have a rule of moral action that is fully adequate to the practical needs of man's moral life, therefore, we need something more. To be specific, we must find some additional formula in whose terms we can decide which among those acts not covered by the Principle are moral and which immoral, a formula that will enable us to determine, for example, when (if ever) the reason 'He's my brother' can justify a discriminatory act and when it cannot. This task will occupy most of Part III.

My main objective in this Part has been to solve the problem of moral justification – of finding a way to support our beliefs about how we ought, as moral beings, to act – by deriving the moral 'ought' from a self-justifying 'ought' – our unescapable obligation to be rational. Just as we cannot justify an irrational belief, our reasons for affirming its truth being equally good reasons for affirming the truth of its denial, so I have argued, we cannot justify performing an arbitrary act, our reasons for doing it being equally good reasons for doing some alternative, incompatible act instead. I should perhaps emphasize that, when I maintain that I have *derived* a moral 'ought' from the rational 'ought', I do not mean that I have *deduced* the one from the other. Had I attempted to argue in that way I would have fallen into the same logical trap that has vitiated most traditional theories of moral obligation. My meaning of derivation is quite different: The moral 'ought' *is* the rational 'ought' applied to a specific kind of context, namely, the practical situation in which human beings perform actions that have consequences affecting the happiness of others.

Although the derivation I have made is, I believe, sound, it does not give a complete account of the grounds on which our moral obligations rest. For actions – I am using the term now in the narrow sense in which it refers to overt physical activities – have a dimension that beliefs in themselves do not. The reason why arbitrary actions are immoral, rather than simply unjustifiable, lies in the fact that they have consequences which affect the happiness of other human beings. This difference between irrational belief and arbitrary action allows us to draw a further distinction. A given belief, if it is irrational, is so necessarily; nothing can be done to divest it of this character. So, too, with an action; if it is unjustifiable, it is so necessarily. There is no contingency in either case. However, that an action be arbitrary (in the special meaning I have given to this term) and hence immoral is contingent. Our characterization of certain acts as immoral results from the nature of the life that we live, hence could disappear under changed conditions of life or of social relationships. For example, if our acts had no effects on the lives of anyone else or if no one cared whether we promoted their happiness or not, my notion of arbitrary action would have no moral significance, but would be morally indistinguishable from what I have called 'gratuitous' action.[9] Even more, the concept of moral obligation itself would simply disappear from our vocabulary.

We must pursue this contingent element in the immorality of arbitrary action in order not only to see where it will lead but also to complete the theory of the moral life I am developing in this essay. Besides completing the theory, our inquiry will lead to a modification of the implication (that our moral obligations extend equally to all individuals affected by what we do) and answer the objection (that the theory provides no criterion by which to determine the morality of many of our acts), that I have noted just above. In very general terms, we can say that the full theory falls into two parts, the first, in which the moral situation is considered from the side primarily of the agent, and a second, in which it is considered from the side primarily of those affected by what the agent does (the 'patients'). So far the moral agent has occupied the centre of the stage and we have, as a result, been making heavy use of the concepts associated with moral action – 'ought', duty, and obligation. But now we shall shift to the other side of the scene and a new moral concept, associated with the 'patients' rather than the agent, will make its appearance – *right* and *rights*. We shall begin Part III with this concept.

NOTES TO PART II

¹ It might be noted that we use other terms to convey the same idea as 'ought'. Two in particular need mention – *duty* and *obligation*. In ordinary discourse, a person normally means the same thing whether he says 'You *ought* to do that act', or 'That act is your *duty*', or 'You have an *obligation* to do that act'. One variation in usage might, however, be mentioned. Although 'obligation', like 'ought', is used in a wide variety of contexts – we speak, for example, of legal obligations, political obligations, and so on – the usage of 'duty' tends to be restricted more closely to moral contexts. But even with it the restriction is by no means complete, the phrase 'social duties', for example, being commonly used. In the remainder of the essay I shall use both terms as equivalent notions to 'ought'.

² The question might well be raised: 'Why not say that happiness is the object of *all* of men's desires?' Then my statement 'All men desire to be happy' might be considered a tautology rather than a generalization. My reason for avoiding this interpretation is that I think that it does not provide a complete account of human motivations. At least two exceptions have to be noted. (1) Sometimes we act so impulsively that, even though we are motivated in what we do by some desire, we do not rise to the level of consciousness in which we view the satisfaction of our desire as contributing to our happiness. Nevertheless, when we deliberate about our acts and make choices among alternatives, if no moral considerations intrude, the question of the contribution which each of the alternatives will make to our happiness is usually not far from the centre of our consciousness. And, most importantly, when we are asked to justify the choices we make, if they are of more than trivial significance, we find ourselves doing so in terms of our 'pursuit of happiness'. (2) To say that we seek happiness in everything we do gives a too strong implication of universal self-centredness in our motivations. Certainly we all seek happiness but that is not the only thing we seek. For most of us have some direct interest in the welfare of others. We are motivated to act at times by the desire that someone other than ourselves should be happy. On the other hand, I think that the generalization 'No one acts in a way that aims at decreasing his personal happiness for its own sake' might with some justice be interpreted as a tautology. Certainly it expresses a well-nigh universal truth.

³ I should note that I am not here defending the thesis that human experience contains ingredients of more value than happiness but am simply attempting to show that the Aristotelian view involves such an implication. If I were asked to defend the philosopher's life

(or any other) as the best possible life for man, I should do so on the grounds that it yielded the *most* happiness of which life can be possessed.

[4] I should note a slight asymmetry between 'irrational' and 'arbitrary', as I use these terms. An irrational belief, as I have defined it, has no necessary social reference but an arbitrary act does. I bring the reference to social consequences into my definition of 'arbitrary' because I shall be using this term in the development of my moral theory. An overt act for which no reasons could be given but whose performance lacks any social significance I would call a gratuitous act. I think that my use of both terms is consistent with normal usage.

[5] i.e. What specific persons . . . ?

[6] There are, naturally, exceptions; for example, we do sometimes act to promote the welfare of someone else without first weighing his claims against those of others. When we do so, our action, because it discriminates between other people without reason, is equally as arbitrary as action in which we pursue our own ends without prior moral deliberation.

[7] Of course, some of our everyday decisions are too trivial in their social consequences to be considered. They are beneath morality. Examples might be our choice from the menu when dining or our decision to take one scenic drive rather than another. And so on. But no rigid line can be drawn between decisions that are moral and those that are not; this is a matter of judgment in the individual situation.

[8] Much less do we seek to diminish our own happiness, a policy that in its extreme would be consistent with disinterested cruelty. (See note 2, p. 59.)

[9] See above, note 4.

III

I SHALL begin this Part by stating a Principle, complementary to that of Personal Impartiality, which I shall call the Principle of Equal Rights. It is quite simple: Every person has an equal right to happiness.

The only explanation this Principle requires, I think, is a brief comment on the term 'right'. Although we all use the term regularly, most of us would be hard put to define it. But this at least we can say: That 'right', in its normal usage without any qualifying adjectives, is a distinctively moral notion and that we use it when we describe a moral situation from the side of the 'patient' rather than that of the agent. Just as we say that a person has a duty to perform a certain act that promotes the happiness of another, so we also say that the other person has a right to have his happiness promoted. Because the first person is under an obligation to him, he can legitimately demand that the obligation be fulfilled.

To justify the Principle of Equal Rights, however, is another matter. What reasons can I give for believing it to be true? Actually I have already answered this question, at least by implication; all that I need to do here is to extend the argument that I presented in Part II, to include the additional concept of 'rights'. The key to my justification of the Principle lies in the following: That happiness can be considered the general object of men's desires, that evaluations of happiness must be made on a strictly quantitative and never a qualitative basis, and that happiness cannot be shared but is an individual possession. The relationship between these conclusions and the Principle of Equal Rights can be elaborated in the following way: Each individual person, in his search for happiness, finds himself in a society of other individuals, all of whom are engaged in the same quest. Although we all desire to maximize our own happiness, we must recognize that in our attempts to do so, we sometimes act in ways that thwart the desires of others. We are then confronted with the moral question of whether we can justify ourselves in pursuing our personal happiness at the expense of that of our fellows. If happiness is an individual possession and if all experiences of happiness are qualitatively on a par, it follows that two experiences of happiness, quantitatively equal but enjoyed by two different individuals, are equally desirable. Neither of the individuals can defend his acting in a way that will realize his own happiness, simply because it is his own, at the expense of that of the other person. For, if he could justifiably act in such a way, so too could the other person. Both would give the same reason for doing what they did but this reason would be used to support two different acts. Furthermore, these acts would be incompatible with each other (in the sense that his performing one of them would preclude an individual at the same time from performing the other) for one would promote the happiness of a certain specific person at the expense of that of another and the second would have the opposite effect. Hence, to pursue one's own or any given individual's happiness at the expense of the equal happiness of any other individual is to act arbitrarily and immorally.

The impossibility of providing any justification for such discriminatory action led me, in Part II, to the Principle of Personal Impartiality. The same impossibility leads me now, looking at the moral situation from the other side, to the Principle of Equal Rights. The reason why I say that every person has an equal right to happiness is that no rational defence can be given in support of action that discriminates between the happiness of different persons on the basis of their individual uniqueness alone. In all our acts we ought to consider the equal happiness of individual persons, whoever they may be, equally. For no one has any more right to happiness than anyone else; we are all born naked.

But I have introduced the notion of equal rights not simply

for the purpose of viewing the moral situation from a different perspective but also to help me to extend and complete the theory of the moral life that I began in Part II. My main objective in this Part will be to accomplish that task; in doing so, however, I shall also attempt to answer the objections that I raised against some of the conclusions I have already reached.

To begin the argument I should like to draw out certain implications of the Principle of Equal Rights. The thesis that everyone has an *equal* right to happiness seems to presuppose the view that we do in fact all have a *right* to happiness. For how could we have an equal right unless we first had a right? Clearly such a conclusion, if correct, is important. Logically speaking, however, it need not be granted. For one could argue that it is quite permissible to hold both that everyone has an equal right to happiness and that no one has any right to happiness at all. The situation would be like that of one beggar telling another that they were equally rich because both were penniless. So my Principle of Equal Rights does not presuppose the thesis that everyone has a right to happiness. Nevertheless, although we cannot directly deduce a universal right to happiness from the Principle of Equal Rights, we can derive it from a combination of the Principle with one further premise; namely, the matter of fact that some individual person is happy. If it be a fact that any person is, or has been, happy and if the Principle of Equal Rights is true, then it follows that every person has a right to happiness. Furthermore, since we all have an equal right to happiness, everyone has a right to be as happy as the happiest man who has ever lived. If we look at the human situation in terms of our rights we find the picture to be an optimistic one indeed; the irony of life, however, lies in the enormous gap, which never seems to narrow, between rights and realizations.

One of the facts of human experience on which I have based the Principle of Equal Rights is the impossibility of drawing qualitative distinctions between experiences of happiness. The idea of 'higher' and 'lower' types of happiness is illegitimate and must be replaced by the quantitative notion of more or less happiness. This fact, combined with the Principle of Equal Rights, produces important consequences that must be examined further. The point can be put by raising the following question: Although we cannot legitimately prefer the happiness of any given person over the equal happiness of any other, is it not permissible to prefer the greater happiness of one over the lesser happiness of another? To make use of an illustration, suppose that by doing a certain act A I could produce a given amount of happiness, distributed equally between persons X and Y. However, by doing another act B I could produce a greater total amount of happiness but this would be enjoyed by X alone. Could I not, consistently with the Principle of Personal Impartiality, argue that I am free to do act B, on the grounds that I would not be discriminating between X and Y on the basis simply of their individual uniqueness but that I could offer an additional reason for my discrimination; namely, that the act I had chosen to do would produce more happiness than its alternative? Although it may seem convincing, this argument contains a problem, which becomes apparent when we return to our illustration. Having attempted to justify act B on the grounds that, even though it discriminates against person Y, it produces more happiness than act A, which is non-discriminatory, what answer can we give to person Y if he asks us why we didn't choose instead to do act C, which would promote a happiness equal to that resulting from act B, but to be enjoyed by Y rather than by X? We find ourselves put by this question back again in the position not only of having discriminated but of having done so arbitrarily. For we can offer no reason for performing act B in preference to act C that would not equally be a reason for performing act C in preference to act B. (And, of course, had we chosen to do act C the situation would have been the same; only in that case the protest would have come from X.)[1]

It is impossible to erase the incompatibility between discriminatory action and the Principle of Equal Rights by an argument that appeals simply to the production of a greater amount of happiness, because we are still left with the question, which we cannot answer, of how that happiness is to be distributed. This conclusion, furthermore, has two important implications. In the first place, it eliminates the possibility of providing any satisfactory account of our moral obligations in utilitarian terms alone. Whatever part the appeal to its better consequences may play in our justification for performing a certain action in preference to some other – and I shall have more to say on this point later – such an appeal cannot override our duty to treat everyone equally. In our moral deliberations justice must precede utility. Secondly, the implication of my argument that we are morally obligated to promote a lesser happiness, equally distributed, to a greater happiness, unequally distributed, is not an easy one to accept. For it appears to come very near, in practice, to precluding us from ever acting in a way that will increase human happiness at all. Since almost any act we perform is bound to discriminate against someone, we seem by this argument to be condemned to perpetual immobility. Or, to put the difficulty in other terms, we seem to be forced logically to embrace the old dictum 'Fiat iustitia, ruat caelum'. Such a conclusion, most people would agree, constitutes a *reductio ad absurdum* of any moral theory. And in this I think they are right. So we cannot rest our case here but must develop our theory further in a manner that will circumvent these implications. The path we must follow, however, is closely circumscribed. Since no answer that violates the Principle of Equal Rights is acceptable, what we must attempt to do is to develop some argument that will allow us to act in a way that discriminates between individuals yet, in doing so, does not violate any person's equal right to happiness.

The solution to our problem lies in the concept of a right itself. Like happiness, a right is an individual's personal possession. In our ordinary thinking and discourse we distinguish various kinds of personal rights – legal, constitutional, traditional, religious, and so on. More importantly for our purposes, we recognize that people have moral rights, of which,

I am arguing, the equal right to happiness is the most basic. Now it is essential to the nature of a right that no other person can, by his own action alone, legitimately deprive an individual of a right that he possesses. For example, if I have a certain legal right, it is illegal for someone else to deprive me of that right. Likewise, to deprive me of my moral rights is immoral. My rights are my own and not to be violated by any outsider. Because they are my own, however, they are at my disposal. I may always legitimately assert them but I may also on occasion waive them. To waive a right is a voluntary act; it is to set the right aside or to suspend it but not to nullify it. All of us frequently waive our rights – for example, in failing to vote on an election day. In like manner we often waive our equal right to happiness. We voluntarily accept a situation in which happiness (or the generally acknowledged means thereto) is unequally distributed to our own detriment. And when we waive our right, those whose acts would (but for the waiver) constitute a violation of that right are released from their moral obligation to respect it. Since they can offer a legitimate reason for ignoring our right, they can discriminate against us with moral impunity, free of any charge of arbitrary action.

The fact that individuals can and do waive their moral rights, although it permits us to sanction discriminatory action without violating our two Principles, provides only a limited solution to the problem we have posed. For it still remains true that each of us must respect every other individual's equal right to happiness unless the other individual in question frees us from our obligation by some act of his own. Since the majority of the individuals whose interests we must consider are people we do not and cannot know personally, we need some additional argument to make the concession we have gained practically significant. To lay the groundwork for this argument will require a further examination into a point I have just made.

I have said that all of us do on occasion waive our equal right to happiness. (There may be a few exceptions to this statement; nevertheless, the fact that it is true of an overwhelming majority of people is sufficient for my purposes.) Almost every day we voluntarily subordinate our own interests, if only in a small way, to those of someone else. Parents sacrifice for their children, teachers for their students, professional men for their clients, and so on. But voluntary acts are performed for some reason. So we may ask: Why do people act in this way? What motivates them to waive their rights so that someone else may enjoy more happiness? It would be impossible to answer this question in specific terms, because the reasons that operate are usually complex and probably different in each individual situation. However, I think we can categorize most of the individual motivations under three main heads. Sometimes people sacrifice their own happiness on moral grounds. Believing that the happiness of some is being bought at the expense of that of others, who have an equal right to happiness, they set about to redress the balance. They are motivated, in other words, by a sense of duty. Anyone who performs an act of self-sacrifice because he believes he owes it to someone else could fall into this category. Again, many times we defer to others not because we believe we have a duty to do so but simply because we want to. We prefer their happiness to our own. Perhaps the best example of such action is furnished by parents who sacrifice themselves for their children, but almost all of us are willing to defer our own happiness to that of someone whom we love or who is our friend.

But there is another reason why we waive our equal right to happiness, quite different from the first two and much more common than either. We waive this right for strategic reasons, because we believe that by doing so we can in the long run promote our own happiness more effectively than we could do by always insisting on the right. In order to explain the apparent paradox – that self-sacrificing action can be reasonably justified in self-interested terms – it is necessary to consider such action in its social context. To do so let us contrast two types of social arrangement. In the first, each member of the society attempts to fulfil the literal requirements of the Principle of Equal Rights in every act he performs and expects that everyone else will do the same. In the second, he does not. Rather he limits his concern to the welfare of people fairly close to him – his family, his friends, his business associates, the members of his immediate community. Nor does he evidence an equal concern for all of these; rather the strength of his interest radiates out like the circles around a pebble dropped into a pond, which become weaker the farther removed they are from the centre. And he assumes that everyone else will act in much the same way. Furthermore, just as he expects the others to waive their rights, so he in turn is willing to waive his. The reason why he waives his personal right, and assumes that the others will waive theirs, is his belief that the result will be the greatest possible happiness for all, including himself, even though he has no guarantee that the happiness will be distributed equally or that he will realize a share equal to that enjoyed by someone else. In other words, he gives up his right to equity in the expectation that, by doing so, (1) he will end up a happier man and (2) others will gain in happiness as well.

Is such a strategem generally successful? Will the individuals who make up our second society have a better chance of happiness than those who constitute our first? Although one cannot answer these questions absolutely, the issue hardly seems in doubt. The very fact that all communities that persist approximate much more closely to our second arrangement than to our first is in itself strong evidence in its favour. But arguments can be given as well. For one thing, it is doubtful whether the kind of social organization that our first alternative pictures could function successfully. For how could each individual in a society, before he acted, take into practical consideration the equal welfare of every individual whose happiness might be affected by what he did? He might be able to do so if he lived in a very small, isolated community, for example, some primitive society or a self-sufficient Utopian colony, like those that were so popular in America in the nineteenth century. But even such societies would be able to achieve their communal moral objective (if they really could do so at all) only by ignoring their obligations to everyone on the outside. In the actual world in which almost all of us find ourselves, to attempt to act in a way that will promote equally the happiness of everyone else is not only to face failure but to contribute less to the welfare of our fellows than we could produce by pursuing more modest aims.

But there is an even further difficulty. Our actions often have consequences that can affect the welfare of future generations. Since the mere fact that a human being is not yet born in no way diminishes his equal right to happiness when he appears on the temporal scene, it in no way diminishes the obligation of those who are now living to take his happiness into consideration when they act. To the extent that their actions will affect his happiness, they are as obligated to him as they are to their contemporaries. Yet they cannot practicably fulfil this obligation. Can anyone answer the question: Just how ought we to act now to insure in the best possible way that each person who may be living in the mid-twenty-fifth century will have an equal share of happiness? The imponderables are so great that any attempt to lay down rules or even to make suggestions (except in extremely general terms) would be quite hopeless. We simply do not know enough about the far-distant future to proceed with any kind of assurance at all.

The conclusion is, I think, clear. Not only is it practically impossible, given the actual conditions of human life, for anyone to act in a way that will satisfy fully the requirements of moral action based on the Principle of Equal Rights but, more importantly, if everyone attempted to do so, the result would almost surely be a substantial diminution in the happiness of all concerned. For no society – and, in particular, none in our complex modern world – could function effectively if people acted in such a way. On the assumption that we are all seeking our own greatest happiness in life, it follows that, if we are intelligent beings as well, we shall by no means always insist on our equal right to happiness. Rather we will realize that we can gain more personal happiness by waiving that right than by always insisting on it. Not only do we promote more effectively the happiness of others by our waiver but more importantly from our point of view we contribute to maximizing our own. On self-interested grounds alone, the waiver of the right presents itself as a good bargain. Certainly it is one that I, if I may speak for myself, am willing to make. To use a specific example, I would not hold the Pilgrims to account if they had no thought for my personal welfare (as an individual who would live three centuries later) as they went about the desperate business of trying to survive their first grim winters in the New World. They had problems enough to face without adding the burden of concerning themselves with the possible consequences of their acts on Americans who might live in the twentieth century. And had they taken our welfare into consideration they would almost surely have miscalculated badly, doing things that would have hurt rather than helped us. For how could they possibly have had any conception at all of what the needs of life would be in twentieth-century America? Yet certain of the decisions they made have had profound effects on the subsequent development of American civilization, some of them very probably impairing the happiness of many generations all the way up to the present time and even beyond. My argument, which I am prepared to back on practical, self-interested grounds, is that these decisions, whatever their errors may have been, should not be faulted on the grounds that they were made without taking into account my personal happiness. Had that happiness been considered, I would almost surely have been the loser. Or, to move from the time to the space dimension, I do not expect every peasant in the interior of China to concern himself with my happiness as he goes about his daily tasks. In the ordinary course of events, there is little he can do to affect that happiness and any attempt he might make would very probably be worse than a failure. Yet we hardly need be reminded that Mao Tze-Tung was reared on a peasant farm in Hunan. Reversing the situation, I would expect that those who will follow us, say, in the twenty-fifth century as well as the peasants of China will respond in the same way that I do, and for the same reason. They will waive their rights and release me from my full obligations, in the conviction that such a response will yield more happiness for them than they could gain from a strict insistence on those rights.[2]

My argument that it is reasonable for someone whose main concern lies in promoting his own welfare to waive his equal right to happiness raises several practical problems. The central thesis of the argument – that the members of a society in which this right is sometimes waived stand a better chance of being happy than those of one in which it never is – is, I think, beyond dispute. But that does not solve our own individual problems. We still must make decisions regarding, for example, the extent to which we shall be willing to waive our rights, the circumstances under which we shall do so, and the people whom we shall relieve of their obligations to us. Assuming that we are both prudential and reasonable, we shall base our decisions on a calculation of the relative gains and losses of personal happiness that they will produce. These calculations, since they require a prediction of future events, are always fallible so any decision we base on them involves a risk. We may discover, too late, that the return we gain for waiving our rights does not compensate us for the sacrifice we have made. Of course, we do not operate in the dark. The accumulated experience of mankind has produced numerous rules that we can apply to our own personal situations to help us in deciding whether it will be to our advantage either to insist upon, or to waive our rights. I shall not take the time here to pursue this matter any further, however, since the problem it concerns, although intensely practical, is one of prudence rather than morality. And my argument raises a moral, as well as a prudential issue, to which I shall now turn.

I began this Part by maintaining that every person has an equal right to happiness. I then pointed out that it is of the nature of a right that the person who possesses it can waive it. In the last few pages I have been discussing the reasons why individuals do waive this right and have argued that the most general reason (which rests on the very nature of man as a being both of reason and desire) is the judgment that his waiver of the right will bring him more happiness than he could gain by a strict insistence on it. But a complication – that should already be apparent from some of the illustrations I have used – now arises. To waive one's right is a voluntary act; no one can perform it except the person who possesses the right. And, unless the waiver is made, everyone else has an obligation to respect the right. Yet I have said that I willingly release the Pilgrims from their strict obligation to consider my happiness and have extended the waiver to peasants in China. I have added, on the other side, that I assume that the Chinese peasants and the possible inhabitants of the earth five hundred years from now will grant me the same concession. But all this is strictly impossible. I cannot waive my rights to the Pilgrims;[3] they have been dead and gone for centuries. No more can my remote descendants waive their rights to me. From the very nature of things we can never meet. The same kind of difficulty, in a less acute form, holds of my moral relationships with the peasants of China. I have never, to my knowledge, met one, nor can I reasonably expect ever to do so.

What, then, can I mean by saying that I waive my rights to the Pilgrims and assume that people of the future will waive their rights to me? Literally understood, the notion is nonsensical; so we must interpret it figuratively. What I am implying is that, if I could, I would (for the prudential reason I have given) waive my rights and that I am assuming that my descendants (for the same reason) would, if they could, waive their rights. The Pilgrims could, in other words, have *legitimately* assumed that I would waive the right and acted accordingly just as I now can do with respect to my descendants. In each case we assume that, even though the other person does not (because he cannot) explicitly grant us the freedom to act without considering his rights, we do have his *tacit consent* to do so. If the conclusions I reached at the end of Part II about the universal scope of our moral obligations are correct, the notion of tacit consent assumes crucial importance for practical morality. Unless we find it to be legitimate, it would appear that we must condemn all successfully functioning societies as necessarily immoral, for all of them accept and operate on it. So we must be quite sure of its legitimacy.

To defend the idea of tacit consent it is necessary only to point out that it is a legitimate extension of the doctrine of moral rights. A right, by its nature, is under the jurisdiction of the person who possesses it; he can, at his wish, either assert it or waive it, as long as his action does not arbitrarily infringe on the equal rights of others. Knowing that people can, and for good reason do, waive their rights, we can legitimately go on to assume that they would, when the same reasons apply, also do so, even though they are unable, because of the limitations of time, space, and so on, actually to perform the voluntary act required. For example, I think I can say in all honesty that, if everything else in our relative historical positions remained unchanged but I was able to enter a time machine that would put me momentarily in Plymouth Colony in 1620, I would give the Pilgrims my consent to go about their daily business without regard to my personal interests. Not only would almost everyone else do the same but the general agreement, in practice, that tacit consent can be assumed in such situations is a necessary condition for the possibility of human social life.

Although it is legitimate, the notion of tacit consent, when it is applied in practice, can be very dangerous. If I make a decision and act in a situation involving social consequences, I have a moral obligation to respect the equal right to happiness of every individual whose interests will be affected by what I do. I can be released from this obligation only if the individuals concerned waive their rights. But – and here arises the danger – they need not actually forego their rights. For I can, and often must, make that decision for them, assuming that they tacitly consent to a waiver of their rights. Not only am I, as agent, faced with the responsibility of making a decision for someone else about his own interests but I am also offered a tantalizing temptation. Since the decision whether to respect or to disregard the rights of others usually involves us in making a choice between promoting our own happiness or theirs, we are, in effect, morally required to decide an issue impartially under conditions in which our natural urges are strongly biased in our own favour. As moral agents we are all constantly placed in the ambivalent situation of having to assume the roles both of advocate and judge, in a case that we usually want very much to win.[4]

We must all make such decisions, for they are the very stuff of our moral life as it is actually lived. How should we, then, decide? What considerations should move us? If someone were to come to us for advice about whether he ought to do a certain act that will promote the welfare of another or to consider himself free to pursue his own interests, what should we tell him? I think we should say that he must try to put himself in the place of the other person and ask whether he would, in that situation, himself waive his right, making sure, when he does so, that he bases his decision on an appreciation of the other person's interests rather than on any attempt to transfer his own desires (which might be quite different) to the other. If he can honestly give an affirmative answer to this question, he can assume the tacit consent of the other person and act accordingly. But such advice, however sound, is probably too general to be of much practical help. We must be more specific, offering him some guidelines in terms of which he can, when he makes his decision on behalf of the other person, reach a conclusion that he has good reason to believe the other person would find acceptable. To provide these we must return to the question: What reasons lead people to waive their equal right to happiness? Earlier in this Part, I suggested three such reasons – a sense of duty, fellow-feeling, and sophisticated self-interest. Of these, the only one I think we can reasonably recommend for use by an agent who is making a decision on behalf of another person is the last. Unless he has explicit assurances to the contrary, a person can assume that someone else would waive his rights only if he believed that such a waiver, by contributing to the general happiness of the society, would yield a greater return in happiness to him than he would have gained by an insistence on those rights. Two considerations lead me to this conclusion: first, that self-interest is in fact the overwhelmingly predominant motive leading people to waive their rights and, secondly, that, because the agent is making the decision on behalf of someone else, it would be highly presumptuous for him to assume that the other person would waive his rights simply as a matter of self-sacrifice (whether from fellow-feeling or from a sense of duty), without any expectation of personal recompense. Although this conclusion is by no means axiomatic, it is, I believe, the only judgment on which we can safely rely, as we go about the serious and difficult business of living the moral life.

My main objective in this Part has been to complete the theory of the moral life that I commenced in Part II. In doing so, however, I have been concerned also to answer a serious objection and to consider further an important implication arising from my argument there. To begin with the objection, at the end of Part II I pointed out that the Principle of Personal Impartiality by itself does not provide an adequate rule for moral action because it is too permissive. Although we can use it to show, for example, that discriminatory acts in which the agent favours some person simply on the grounds of his individual uniqueness are not morally justifiable, we cannot by appealing to it alone reach a decision about the moral status of acts that he might do for certain other reasons. For instance, one can consistently with the Principle justify his discriminating in favour of (or against) another on the grounds that the person is his brother or that he is a total stranger. Even further, it permits as a legitimate ground for discrimination such apparently irrelevant reasons as 'He is red-headed', and so on.

For these reasons the Principle of Personal Impartiality needs to be supplemented. I have provided the necessary supplementation in the Principle of Equal Rights, and the implications I have drawn from it. Because everyone has an equal right to happiness we all have a moral obligation to respect that right and hence to refrain from arbitrary discrimination against any individual. We can be released from our obligation and practise discrimination without acting arbitrarily only if the person who directly suffers as a result gives his consent, either explicitly or tacitly, to our doing so. If he waives his right explicitly, he can of course do so for any reason that he wishes, within the limitations set by his own moral obligations to others. If, however, we make the decision for him, assuming his tacit consent to a waiver of his right, then we can do so only after we have honestly answered the question 'Would he, given the decision, waive his right for this reason?'

In this question we have supplied a criterion of relevancy which distinguishes between kinds of reasons that can legitimately be offered in favour of discriminatory action (like 'He's my brother') and those that cannot (like 'He's red-headed'). Except in most unusual circumstances, we cannot honestly decide on behalf of someone else that he would willingly consent to waive his equal right to happiness because he has red hair; on the other hand, we can normally assume in our society that we have the tacit consent of everyone to give preference to members of our own family over outsiders. These are, of course, only generalizations; nepotism, for example, is far from a morally neutral epithet. The argument I have given in this Part, furthermore, clarifies the nature of moral deliberation. Our problem, when we consider performing an act that will have discriminatory consequences, must always be to establish that we are not acting arbitrarily. This we can do only if we can provide adequate reasons for concluding that those against whom the act will discriminate would, either explicitly or tacitly, waive their equal right to happiness.

This argument answers a related criticism of my theory, which I raised earlier in this Part, as well. The objection was directed against my conclusion that, since no increase in total happiness could ever justify us in practising discrimination because all discrimination is arbitrary, we must treat everyone with exact equality, whatever the consequences. 'Fiat iustitia, ruat caelum.' The way in which we can avoid this implication should by now be clear. To the extent that the practice of justice does lead to the drastic results suggested in the quotation, no one desires it. For we all want to be happy. Given the choice of suffering from an unequal distribution of happiness in which he nevertheless gains a reasonable amount for himself, or enjoying an equality of happiness in which everyone, himself included, is miserable, almost everyone will without hesitation opt for the first alternative. On this fact the entire notion of tacit consent, which eliminates the arbitrariness from discriminatory action, rests. When we must make a moral decision and are convinced that a strict policy of non-discrimination will have disastrous consequences, we are morally justified in supporting the heavens and letting 'justice' fall.[5] For we can assume that we are acting with the consent of all whose rights must be deferred. And this assumption gives us a reason for discriminating that rescues our action from the charge of being arbitrary.

Finally, a remark about the extent of our moral obligations. An important implication of the Principle of Personal Impartiality, we found in Part II, is that we all labour under an arduous, almost limitless obligation – before we act to consider equally the happiness of every individual who might be affected by what we do. Since we can never draw a line capable of marking the boundary of any act's consequences, we can never decide beyond question that we are morally free to act in disregard of the happiness of anyone who is now alive or may ever live. The theory of tacit consent mitigates this obligation by drawing at least one boundary for us. For we can now say that, if our attempt to consider an individual's interests before we act will lead to a sufficient decrease in his happiness, we have his tacit consent to set those interests aside. Thus the Pilgrims had my tacit consent not to concern themselves with my personal welfare and I assume that I have the same consent from my remote descendants. So limits can be set to the extent of our moral obligations. But our responsibilities, as moral agents, remain unchecked. For the decisions that set limits on our obligations are not ordinarily made by others, consulting their own self-interest, but by us, tempted by ours. These decisions, therefore, must, if they are to be morally acceptable, be scrupulously honest.

At the end of the last Part, I said that in Part III I would shift my perspective, to view the moral situation from the side of the 'patient' rather than that of the agent. The result has been the Principle of Equal Rights, and its implications, which have both modified and completed the moral theory that I have been developing in this essay. However, I have made a second shift in this Part – from an emphasis on the 'ideal' to an emphasis on the 'practical'. The two words I have just used are so notoriously ambiguous that I hesitate to employ them; yet they do most aptly describe the change of emphasis in my arguments. To be specific, in this Part I have taken into account certain facts about the nature of the world and man that are relevant to the moral decisions we must make every day which I did not consider in Part II. Although the theory developed in Part II depends to some degree on the nature of the world and man, its major conclusion (the Principle of Personal Impartiality) is supported primarily through the application of logical considerations to the realm of moral action. And logic is 'ideal', in the sense that no fact can affect a conclusion that has been logically demonstrated. Demonstrable truths remain unchanged, whatever the nature of the world or man may be. In another sense also my conclusions in Part II may be described as 'ideal'. For the Principle of Personal Impartiality applies to what can be called 'limiting cases'. In this respect, it is to some extent analogous to 'ideal' formulations of physical laws. Just as no body in the universe moves in the way that Newton describes in his First Law of Motion (because all are influenced by the force exerted on them by other bodies) so it is probably near the truth to say that no person who seriously deliberates before he acts has as his only reason for the decision he makes the individual uniqueness of the persons who will benefit from what he does. Nevertheless, in both situations the 'ideal' formulations perform an important function. Newton's law demands that we find an explanation for the observed behaviour of any given body in terms of the forces exerted on it by other bodies. And the Principle of Personal Impartiality demands that we find a justification for our discriminatory acts through an appeal to considerations other than the personal uniqueness of the individuals whose happiness is affected by what we do.

When we turn to practical morality we find that the limitations imposed by the actual conditions under which we must live and act require us to supplement the Principle of Personal Impartiality, founded on the requirements of logic. Although the Principle of Personal Impartiality, founded on the requirements of logic. Although the Principle lays down an absolute moral injunction against arbitrary action, hardly anyone who acts on reflection in fact ever acts completely arbitrarily.[6] Yet we all regularly act in a discriminatory way. So the central problem for practical ethics is to find a means by which we can distinguish between discriminatory action that is arbitrary and hence immoral and discriminatory action that is not. This I have attempted to do in Part III, with the Principle of Equal Rights and the implications I have drawn from it.

These conclusions corroborate a generalization of long standing in ethics – that an adequate theory of the moral life must rest on an appeal to both reason and practical experience. It cannot defy reason, for then it would be doomed from the start. But it cannot rest on reason alone, for it must answer questions whose solutions depend on contingent facts, for example, that man is in part a creature of desires, that the desires of different individuals come into conflict, that our knowledge (particularly of the future and of the desires of others) is very limited, and that most people will forego their claim to equity if they can by doing so realize a substantial increase in happiness. The implications of these contingent facts we learn by experience and to cope with them we must appeal to experience. As a result, our practical moral decisions can never have the rigour of the logician's deductions. To live and to act is to sail a dangerous sea and there is no port to which one can safely retire.

NOTES TO PART III

[1] The illustration I have used assumes that I can perform either of two alternative acts, one favouring person X and the other

favouring person Y. In actual fact, this is usually true (although my illustration necessarily oversimplifies the conditions in which we normally must act). In circumstances in which it is not true, no moral problem of the type I pose need arise.

² I do not mean to over-state my case here. We are by no means released by my argument from all obligations to future generations. For we *can* increase their happiness by considering their rights – up to a point. All that I am suggesting is that a point is reached beyond which our attempts to take their welfare into consideration will constitute a hindrance rather than a help to their happiness. Of course, it is impossible in practice to know in any specific case just when that point is reached. We must simply use our best judgment and act accordingly.

³ The terminology I use here ('I waive my right to someone') is elliptical but convenient. Strictly speaking, I mean 'I waive my right and thus release someone from the obligation of respecting that right'.

⁴ The notions of the waiver of rights and of tacit consent raise additional problems in actual practice that a full treatise on practical morality, which my essay is not, would have to consider. To mention one example: Can we conclude that someome has really waived his right even if he has in fact given it up, when he lives under conditions that preclude him from fully understanding and appreciating his possession of that right? Because many Negroes in the South voluntarily accepted slavery, were the white people justified in treating them as slaves? In situations like this the answer would have to be that the factual waiver is not a true waiver because it was extracted by coercion, the coercion involved in not giving people the opportunity to realize what their rights as human beings are.

⁵ My reason for placing the term 'justice' in quotation marks here is that at this stage in the argument justice need no longer be identified with absolute equity. Conceived abstractly, the two terms are equivalent; however, after it has been established that people willingly waive their right to equity, the incompatibility between justice and discriminatory action disappears. To the extent that an act can be defended in the kinds of terms I have set forth, even though it is discriminatory, it must be granted to be just.

⁶ My statement here is a qualified one, for a reason. I have inserted the adverb 'completely' because I believe that we must, if we are candid, admit that, even though few people who deliberate

about what they do fail completely to take into account the rights of others, almost all of us are to a degree biased in our decisions. The happiness of some – and, in particular, one – is given more weight in our deliberations than that of others, simply because it is their – or our own – happiness. To the extent that this is true, our actions fall short of the moral ideal.

IV

I SET out at the beginning of this essay to solve an important but limited problem – to discover a way of justifying our beliefs about how we ought, as moral beings, to act. The course of my argument has, however, taken me well beyond my initial objective. For I found that, to solve my original problem, I had to answer the much more general question 'How *ought* we as moral beings to act?' Two reasons compelled me to broaden the scope of my inquiry. On the one hand, it is impossible to justify all of our beliefs about how we ought to act because some are simply insupportable; therefore no attempt to solve the problem of moral justification abstractly, in isolation from the specific beliefs we hope to support, can be successful. But this conclusion raises a further problem. If we must, in order to justify certain moral beliefs, know which ones are justifiable, then we must already have solved the problem of moral justification. We are, in other words, trapped by our methodology in a circular argument. To escape the circle – and this was my second consideration – it is necessary to examine the questions 'How ought we to act?' and 'Why ought we to act in this way?' not separately but together. If we can give an answer to the first that is capable of providing an answer to the second as well, we can succeed both in establishing which of our various moral beliefs are theoretically supportable and in providing for these beliefs the argument which constitutes their support. This I have attempted to do in the preceding two Parts. So my essay, which began with the problem of moral justification, has developed into a treatise on the moral life for man.

In this final Part I should like to do two things: Raise and answer certain objections to the theory I have presented and draw out some practical implications that follow from that theory. As a preface to the discussion I should make a remark on the brevity of my essay on man's moral life. Because it is so short, it does not and cannot cover its subject matter in full detail. Rather than writing a voluminous treatise dealing with every facet of the moral life, I have chosen instead to concentrate on the essential features of its logical structure. Nevertheless, if the conclusions I have reached are sound, they provide a theoretical foundation from which a full, detailed account of human morality can be elaborated and in terms of which our practical moral problems can, to the extent that they are soluble, be solved.

Now, to some criticisms of my theory. Certain philosophers would undoubtedly object to the method I have employed in my argument in Part II, contending that it is impossible to reach and defend answers to substantive ethical questions by an appeal to considerations of logic alone. In reply I would point out that my case does not rest exclusively on logical grounds but also on an analysis of the nature of man and the human situation; nevertheless it is true that an appeal to logical considerations is an essential and crucial element in my argument. For I maintain that we all have a demonstrable moral obligation to act in a certain way because the denial of this obligation forces one into a contradiction. The moral 'ought' is, for me, a special case of the logical 'ought'. So I must meet the objection to my methodology squarely.

The first point that should be noted is that the criticism can be raised in both a general and a specific way. Let us consider each in turn. Some philosophers would argue the general case that the reason why substantive ethical issues cannot be resolved by appeals to logic is that no substantive issues of any kind can be resolved in such a way. Since a full-scale refutation of this objection would involve me in a lengthy digression taking us far from the field of moral philosophy and since I have discussed the issue in detail elsewhere, I shall content myself here simply with a brief summary statement of my reply to it. The objection, stated in this general way, must fail because it is logically unsupportable. Anyone who claims that no substantive conclusion can be supported by logical arguments alone, if he is to make his case, finds himself forced into the position of having to assert a substantive conclusion for which nothing but logical arguments can be given. To support his case, thus, he must deny it, so ending in self-contradiction. We can conclude therefore that our assurance that it is possible to solve substantive problems by an appeal to logical considerations alone rests on the firmest of all grounds – that we can demonstrate this possibility.

Although the general objection to my methodology can be disposed of decisively, the specific objection is harder to meet. Here the critic, although he admits that some types of substantive conclusions can be adequately supported by logical arguments alone, denies that these include conclusions about our moral obligations of the type I reached in Part II. The only way in which I could answer a critic of this kind would be to lead him through the steps of my argument again and convince him that my case is sound. Since I have already presented that argument to the best of my ability, to repeat it here would be redundant. So I refer such a critic back to Part II.

A second criticism of my methodology, of a quite different kind, needs to be considered. In Part I I argued that the attempt to justify our moral beliefs by an appeal to intuition ends in failure. In developing my own theory, therefore, I tried to avoid resting my case in any way on such an appeal. But did I succeed? It might be charged against me that at each step in my argument I had to appeal to intuition for, unless I did so, I would never be able to know that the conclusion I reached really followed from the premises from which I had derived it. For example, my conclusion in Part II that action which discriminates between persons on the basis of their individual uniqueness alone is arbitrary rests on the insight, which can be apprehended only by intuitive means, that no grounds can be found in the separate individuality of a person capable of justifying our treating him in a discriminatory way.

To answer this criticism it is necessary to begin with a distinction, between different kinds of intuition. The intuitionism that I criticized in Part I can be called *moral* intuitionism, for it holds that we directly apprehend the truth of moral propositions, like 'Promises, as such, ought to be kept'. But there are other forms of (alleged) intuition, the aesthetic intuition of the artist who directly apprehends the beauty of a painting or the religious intuition of the mystic who directly confronts God. In addition there is the intuition of logical necessity, which occurs, for example, when someone directly apprehends that, if A implies B and B implies C, A must imply C. Returning to my own theory, it is obvious that I appealed to intuition in my argument, if by that is meant that I based my conclusions on some appeal to what I directly apprehended. How could I do otherwise? The concession is innocuous because knowledge, by its very nature, involves intuition. We cannot know anything unless we directly apprehend something. The critical question is not, Do I appeal to intuition? but rather, To what kind of intuition do I appeal? My reply is that I do not appeal to *moral* intuition to support my case. Rather, my alternative is an appeal to the intuition of *logical necessity*. The conclusions I reach about our moral obligations, for example, that we ought not to discriminate between persons on the basis of their individual uniqueness alone, are true, I contend, because they are logically unavoidable. To apprehend this fact, no moral intuitions but only logical intuitions are necessary. Furthermore, although intuition is necessary to apprehend the truth of such conclusions, they are true not because they are intuited in some way, but because they are logically necessary. Finally, an ethical theory based on the appeal to logical necessity can meet and answer all the objections that have been raised with such devastating effects against traditional ethics and at the same time provide a basis for the moral life. It is a new departure in moral philosophy but one which, I am convinced, can be successful.

Turning now to quite a different kind of criticism, I believe that some readers may be disturbed by what appears to be a discrepancy between the conclusions I reached in Parts II and III. After asserting the bold thesis that each of us has a moral obligation to promote equally the happiness of all, I then, it may seem, proceeded to whittle away at my own case until my original contention was so compromised as to lose both its force and character, leaving me to embrace a conception of practical morality that even the most complacent could accept with equanimity. I would respond to this point by emphasizing an important distinction. Although it is quite true that the demands of morality as I stated them originally in Part II and as I finally qualified them in Part III differ considerably from each other, this discrepancy in my conclusions about our moral obligations does not imply any inconsistency within my theory. Rather it is a consequence of the conditions of human life as we actually find it to be. If we or the world were sufficiently different from what we now are, the discrepancy would diminish and could, conceivably, disappear. The ideal and the actual would coalesce.

As far as my theory is concerned, the most important consideration is that it not be guilty of inconsistency. In its defence I would repeat that none of the qualifications I make in Part III obliterates the original obligation that each of us has to promote equally the happiness of all. We cannot, by any act of our own, eliminate it. We can be freed from our responsibility to fulfil the obligation only by an act of the individual to whom we owe it – when he waives his equal right to happiness. And, as I said before, to waive a right is not to destroy it but only to set it aside. But what about the doctrine of tacit consent? Do we not, according to it, ourselves make the decision that relieves us of our obligations to others? In fact, we of course do, because we have to, but in doing so we are (or should be) making the decision not in terms of our own interests but on behalf of those of the other person. We simply act as proxy for him. There is no point in denying that we have the opportunity, and are faced with a great temptation, to disregard his rights, repudiate our obligations, and act to serve our own interests. But that is only to admit – what we all know – that it is easy to act immorally. And it does not alter the fact that our obligation remains, unless he waives his right himself or we, for reasons that he would accept, do so in his behalf. Theoretically, therefore, there is no inconsistency between my original thesis and my final conclusion.

But a practical discrepancy does exist, a result of the difference between what might be possible in some other world and what is possible in the actual world in which we live. This discrepancy can be made clear by an extreme illustration. If every individual has an equal right to happiness, then the Pilgrims had as much right to be happy as I have, and I have as much right to be happy as my descendants have. Now, before I act I must consider my descendants and make a decision, which I must be prepared to defend, that I can reasonably assume that they would, if they could, waive their rights to me, thus permitting me to disregard my obligations to them. And I would hold that the Pilgrims ought to have done the same with respect to me. But the argument does not work in the reverse direction. I do not have to waive my rights in order to release my descendants from any moral obligations to me, nor do the Pilgrims have to waive their rights in order to release me from any moral obligations to them. The simple fact of the irreversibility of time, thus, has profound effects on men's moral relationships to each other. Even though people who came before us in history had as much right to happiness as we who are now living do, and as those who are to follow after us will have, because our acts, by the very nature of time, can affect the happiness only of the latter, our obligations are limited to them.

In many other, less extreme ways people's practical obligations are limited by what they are able to do. We have learned by experience that we do not gain a maximum of happiness in the most efficient way by demanding that everyone whose acts can affect our welfare treat us equally but rather by developing a type of social arrangement in which most individuals limit their major concern to a fairly small circle of those immediately around them. Hence we are willing both to waive our rights and to recognize that others can legitimately assume our tacit consent to such a waiver. If, however, the world were to change in such a way that we could more efficiently promote the happiness of all, ourselves included, by an equal attention to the rights of each, the moral situation would be altered correspondingly. People would no longer be willing to waive their rights and our obligations would, as a consequence, begin to approximate in actual fact what they are in the original formulation of my theory. This point, again, can be illustrated quite easily. Because our practical obligations are limited in large measure by the fact that we can neither calculate nor control the long-range consequences of our actions, an improvement in our ability to do these things would have an effect on our moral responsibilities. The further into the future that we can make accurate predictions and exercise control over the course of events, the greater our moral obligations to our descendants. Thus science and technology, our most effective instruments for accomplishing these ends, play a vital role in the moral life of man. As science develops, our moral obligations expand.

To turn to another set of criticisms, the fact that my theory first states an 'ideal' moral requirement, which it later modifies to make it applicable to the practical exigencies of the human situation, lays it open to attack from two different sides. I shall consider here two pairs of criticisms, in each of which the objection comes first from one direction and then from its opposite.

The first type of criticism concerns my views regarding the scope and character of our duties. On the one side, some would contend that my conclusions about how we ought to act are so impersonal that they violate many of our most deeply-held moral convictions. To say that we have a duty to promote the happiness of all equally – whether they be friends or strangers, live now or five hundred years hence – is to fail to recognize the *special* weight of the obligations we owe to those near to us – our families, friends, fellow-countrymen, and so on. In response I would point out, first, that the kind of practical moral life that I advocate for the average person is, in the respect now being considered, not really unlike that urged by my critics. As I have already said, most of us at the practical level of our daily living ought to be concerned primarily with the welfare of a fairly small group of people immediately around us and only secondarily with those outside this circle. My disagreement with most of such critics lies not in a serious difference of opinion regarding the kind of moral activity I recommend for the ordinary person and the kind that they advocate but rather in the reasons we give in support of this activity. Those who maintain that we have 'special' obligations to certain individuals must be able to provide reasons to justify their stand. This most of them attempt to do by an argument that rests finally on an appeal to some form of moral intuition, a kind of justification that I believe to be inadequate to the task. Rather, if ordinarily-accepted patterns of moral action are to be justified it must be through a quite different kind of argument. I have tried to provide such an argument in the theory I have developed in this essay. Although my purpose has not been to defend ordinary morality, my view does in fact account for the greater obligations we owe to those who are close to us, both in space and time, over those who are far away, something that the traditional appeal to 'special' obligations cannot do.

But this conclusion leads us right into the sights of the critics waiting to attack on the opposite side. My views, they will say, are *too* compatible with ordinary morality. For I do not advocate a way of life that is novel or challenging; in the end, the weight of my argument supports the moral *status quo*. I must give two answers to this charge, one addressed to moral philosophers and the other to the world at large. First, my views about the way in which men ought to act are, I think, in general agreement with the conclusions reached by many ethicists in the Western tradition. My dispute with these philosophers is not on practical but on theoretical grounds. I accept their conclusions but I reject the arguments they advance in support of those conclusions. As I said at the very outset, a study of the major traditional ethicists forces one to conclude not only that they have failed to provide any satisfactory theoretical justification for the conclusions they reach about man's moral life but even further that they present no arguments capable of supporting the belief that men have any duties at all. My primary concern has been to develop a theory that can overcome these deficiencies, by the employment of an entirely new type of argument. In this essay I have attempted to give such an argument, and any claim to novelty that I would make must rest on that.

To the world at large, however, I would emphasize that the conclusions I reach about the moral life by no means imply an unqualified approval of conventional morality. Although I would agree in many instances with the moral views of thoughtful, concerned people (e.g. on the practical scope of our obligations), I find no grounds in my theory for accepting conventional morality *per se*. On the contrary, I think that my two Principles are incompatible with many moral beliefs and practices that have been widely accepted in our society. For example, I do not believe that the practice of discrimination, which through the centuries has caused suffering and unhappiness to millions of human beings, on the basis of differences in religious conviction could be justified by an appeal to my Principles. Nor would these Principles provide any more support for discrimination based on differences in race or colour. Yet both have been defended on moral grounds. If the conclusions about the moral life that follow from my theory are true, many of the conventionally-accepted practices of our society must be judged immoral. I would, therefore, deny that the general acceptance of a certain practice is any guarantee of its moral worth. Not only can morals not be derived from mores but our mores are themselves in need of continuing moral reform.

The next criticism I shall consider, which is also a two-sided one, is aimed not directly against my theory but against certain types of view in ethics of which mine might be considered an example. Any ethical theory, if it is complete, will either state or imply some rule of action that a person can apply to his concrete moral problems in order to decide what he ought to do. One of the ways in which such rules of moral action can be distinguished from each other is in terms of their relative degree of 'subjectivity' or 'objectivity'. The twin criticisms of my theory that I am concerned with here are the charge, that some might make, that the rule of action it sets up is too subjective and the counter-charge, that others might make, that its rule is too objective. Before we can turn to an examination of these objections, however, we must take some time to clarify what I mean by the terms, subjective and objective. Perhaps the best way to explain how I shall be using them is by reference to traditional theories which set up rules of moral action that exemplify each.

Of the major theories of the moral life in the Western tradition, one that lays down a decidedly objective rule of moral action is hedonistic utilitarianism, particularly in the version of it given by Jeremy Bentham. If one were to ask Bentham what kind of acts he ought to do, the reply would immediately come back: Always maximize pleasure. In its appeal to the pleasure we produce by our acts, hedonism sets up an objective standard of moral action, in the sense that one's decisions about what he ought to do depend not on something internal to the person who must make them – his attitudes, aspirations, urges, feelings, and so on – but on something quite external to him – the amount of pleasure that will result from his act. With the aid of the 'hedonistic calculus' and the predictive control of the environment provided by modern science, a hedonist today can feel himself relieved of a great load of personal responsibility in reaching decisions about what his duties are. Little need be left to his subjective judgment; rather he can approach the ideal, which Bentham anticipated, of reading his moral obligations off a computing machine.[1] Perhaps the best contrast to the objectivism of hedonism is the strong tradition in Western moral philosophy that may be termed, somewhat loosely, 'the ethics of conscience'. Although there have been numerous variations on the theme, the basic position can be put quite simply. To the question 'What ought I to do?' the answer is

'Follow the dictates of your conscience'. The subjectivism implicit in this advice lies in the fact that, in order to decide what he ought to do, one does not turn outward, to some feature of the world independent of himself, but inward, to some 'faculty' of his own conscious life.[2]

So much for the meanings of the terms, subjective and objective, as I shall be using them. I now turn to the criticisms of my theory, beginning with the charge that its rule of moral action is too subjective. But again I must pause to make some preliminary remarks. To criticize a theory on the grounds that it is too subjective implies that subjectivism is a fault, and someone might well ask: What is wrong with a subjective rule of action? I shall answer this question by a brief consideration of the ethics of conscience. (Although other forms of subjectivism are not subject to quite the same criticisms as those I shall raise against the ethics of conscience, they all have approximately parallel weaknesses.) If someone asks me what he ought to do and I reply to him 'Always act conscientiously' I have not yet given him any practical moral help. For I have, in effect, told him that he ought to do what he believes he ought to do and, if he was serious in requesting my advice, he was already planning to do that. What he is asking of me rather is to tell him what act, in the particular situation in which he finds himself, is the act a person doing what he ought to do would in fact do and also, perhaps, how he should go about determining what that act is. The appeal to conscience, if it is to have any practical significance, must thus imply more than just that we ought always to do what we believe we ought to do. This the conscience theorists usually recognize, arguing that our conscience, in addition to telling us to act conscientiously, gives us specific and unquestionable information about the act we ought to perform in a given situation. We ask our conscience what we ought to do and it answers 'Do thus and so'.

Setting aside all criticisms of such a view based on objections to the conception of human nature on which it rests – a subject that has been more than adequately covered by others – I shall limit myself to one point. Because the decision about what we ought to do, according to the conscience theory, rests on the dictates of an inner 'faculty' of the individual, *any* act that is so dictated becomes our duty. The result is that we are left with no satisfactory criterion in terms of which we can decide that a given act is moral or immoral. For example, two different individuals, both appealing to conscience, often come to incompatible decisions about what one of them ought to do; the same thing frequently happens to a single person when he makes successive appeals to his own conscience. We find ourselves, thus, facing the problem of whether the person ought to do act A, which his conscience dictates or act B (incompatible with A), which his friend's conscience dictates. Or, again, we are faced with the problem of whether he ought to do act A, which his conscience dictates at time t_1, or act B, which his conscience dictates at time t_2. And even if no such contradictions in fact occurred, it is always possible that they might do so. In such situations, one or the other of the dictates that conscience asserts is demanding that he perform an act which, because it runs directly contrary to a dictate of conscience, must, in the terms of the conscience theory itself, be immoral. But if conscience can and does dictate acts that are immoral, then no appeal to it can provide an acceptable answer to the question: What ought one to do?[3]

There is a way open to conscience theorists by which they might answer this objection. For they could argue that appeals to conscience cannot conflict with each other because the act one ought to do is always and only the act his own conscience dictates to him at the moment of moral decision. Whether the conscience of another, or his own conscience at another time, disagrees with this dictate is irrelevant to what he ought to do. But this line of argument has certain implications that must be noted. According to it, we cannot determine from considering the nature of an act someone has performed – whether it be the sacrificing of his happiness for a friend, the helping of a stranger in distress, or the slaughter of an innocent – if that act is or is not an act he ought to have done. We must make our judgment, rather, on the basis of whether the act, *whichever it be*, was dictated to the agent by his conscience. On this interpretation of the conscience theory, the notion of the moral life, as a life exemplifying certain kinds of actions rather than others, becomes meaningless. For morally *anything* goes. But the conclusion that anything goes – that any action can be equally as moral as any other – is equivalent to moral nihilism.

To avoid the disaster of moral nihilism most conscience theorists have recognized the need to find some way of guaranteeing that the acts conscience dictates will be moral. If conscience is to be our guide, they realize, conscience must be prevented from going astray. The standard traditional solution to the problem has been an appeal to God. Conscience will dictate only what is morally acceptable because it is the voice of God speaking through us. To examine this theory in detail would be beside our purpose, so I shall make just two remarks. To appeal to God is, in effect, to abandon the conscience theory because it is to admit that an act is rendered our duty not because our conscience has dictated it but rather because God, speaking through our conscience, has done so. In turn, it is an abandonment also of the subjectivism (in my sense of the term) of the appeal to conscience in favour of objectivism, for God (according to this hypothesis) is a being who is considered to be external to and independent of the agent who is making the moral decision.

My criticisms of the ethics of conscience have led me into a somewhat lengthy argument but I think the digression is justified if it reveals the pitfalls awaiting anyone who attempts to found a rule of moral action on the dictates of conscience, or, for that matter, on any appeal to an internal 'faculty', attitude, or response of the individual person who is making a moral decision. The end of the line for all such subjectivistic theories is moral nihilism.

With this conclusion in mind, we can return to our main question: Is the rule of action that my theory establishes too subjective? Or, perhaps better, just where does my rule fall on a scale that runs from extreme subjectivism to extreme objectivism? It is fairly easy to give a general answer to this question; however, it will be necessary to make some qualifications and further explanations on points of detail. According to my theory, an individual trying to decide what act he ought to do must always base his decision essentially on a factor that is independent of his own feelings, urges, attitudes, or responses and hence is objective to him as an individual – the happiness that will result from what he does. Like the hedonists, who say that we ought to maximize pleasure, I say that we ought to maximize happiness, with the crucial provision that we ought to distribute this happiness equally among all whom our acts will affect. Thus my theory falls, like hedonism, on the objective side of the scale. Yet it is not so objective as Bentham's view; even though I maintain that differences in happiness must be judged in purely quantitative terms, I hold forth no prospect that we shall ever be able to solve our moral problems by a computing machine. The reason for my pessimism on this score lies in the great difference between happiness and pleasure. Although pleasure is a complex phenomenon of man's conscious life – much more so, I believe, than Bentham realized – it is relatively simple in comparison to happiness. So the question 'How much pleasure can I produce by doing this act?' is incomparably easier to answer than the question (setting aside for the moment the problem of the equitable distribution of happiness) 'How much happiness can I produce?' On the theory I have presented, the moral agent has to shoulder a much heavier responsibility than the person following the hedonistic view. Hence his decisions will contain a greater subjective element than those of the hedonist. In mitigation of this difference I would argue that the adequacy of a rule of moral action is not determined solely by its objectivity. On the contrary, hedonism purchases objectivity at too high a price, by asking us to determine what we ought to do by reference to a standard that rests on an impoverished conception of human nature and the goals men seek in life.

Because each of us must assume the serious responsibility of calculating the amount and distribution of the happiness that will result from our performing a variety of alternative acts in order to reach a decision about what we ought to do, it is inevitable that subjective considerations will influence our judgment. Nevertheless, we should do our best to minimize such influences. Let me explain more specifically. When we ask ourselves before we act 'What ought I to do to promote the happiness of others?' we are often prone to answer in terms of our own experience, concluding that what would make us happy will make others happy too. Such a method is by no means unreasonable if we are sufficiently like other people in our wants and desires that what would satisfy us will satisfy them as well. If, however, our needs are idiosyncratic, we cannot make them the standard for our action. Most importantly, we must always remember that it is someone else's happiness, not ours, with which we are concerned. When possible, we should try to find out from them what they believe will best promote that happiness. For each person is his own final judge about his own happiness. We can counsel him, argue with him, and try to persuade him to change his ways if we believe he is pursuing a path of folly, but we cannot legislate his happiness for him; he must make his own mistakes. In situations in which we cannot consult the individuals concerned, we should turn to whatever sources of help we can find, for example, history and the experience of mankind. And certainly our own experience can be valuable, if we are careful to make judicious use of it and refrain from indiscriminately universalizing our own wants, desires, and idiosyncracies.

A final remark on subjectivism. Although no ethical theory that is worth serious consideration can completely avoid all elements of subjectivism (for the moral agent must be left with some personal responsibility in making his decisions), the crucial issue is whether or not this subjective element is embedded in the rule of action the theory sets up. In conscience theories (and other forms of subjective appeal) it is. To reach a decision about what he ought to do, a person is logically forced to turn inward. In my theory, however, he is not. For he can make his moral decisions without ever consulting his internal consciousness, by concluding on the basis of objective evidence that a certain act will promote an optimum distribution of happiness.

In replying to the charge that the rule of moral action which my theory lays down is too subjective, I have in part answered the opposite side of the criticism – that the rule is too objective. However, I have not met this objection fully because those who would make it would probably have a quite specific complaint to level against my theory, namely, that its rule of action is absolute. And for some absolutism in ethics is anathema. In one sense I would agree with such critics. Because there is no rule we can apply that is capable of providing us with unquestionable answers to our practical moral problems, I do not believe that any concrete moral decision we make can be infallible. But I have made ample allowance in my theory for the essential fallibility of our practical moral decisions. Whenever we act, if we act morally, we base our decision about what we ought to do on a judgment regarding the amount of happiness our action will produce and the manner in which that happiness will be distributed. Our decision, thus, must rest on a calculation of imponderables. Even though we do the best we can, bringing into our deliberations the whole weight of past experience and the predictive machinery of empirical science, we can still make mistakes. Hence no specific moral command can ever be absolute.

Such a fallibilistic conclusion, however, is in no way incompatible with the thesis that a rule of moral action, like my Principle of Personal Impartiality, may be absolute. It can be argued, on the contrary, that a rule, if it is really to function as such, must be absolute. Certainly those set up by most moral philosophers have been so. To mention just one example: According to the hedonists, one ought always to act in such a way as to maximize pleasure and minimize pain. This rule is absolute; no exceptions to it are morally allowable. Yet the hedonists, even with Bentham's calculus, must admit that any practical decision we make, because it involves a calculation of the consequences of our acts, is subject to error, hence that no absolute commands can, at this level, be laid down.

When one considers a rule of moral action, like my Principle of Personal Impartiality or the hedonists' Principle of Utility or any other, the critical issue is not, Are these rules absolute? but rather, Can these rules be justified by argument? If not, they must be judged to be arbitrary. Such a judgment, which is philosophically fatal, must, I believe, be rendered against the rules embodied in the theories of most traditional moral philosophers. If the argument of this essay is sound, however, the rule that my theory sets up succeeds in escaping it.

The final criticism of my theory I shall consider concerns a logical point. By applying my Principles, it may be admitted, a conscientious moral agent can find an answer – fallible, to be sure – to the question 'What act ought I to do in this particular situation?' but he cannot use them to reach an answer to the more general and logically more basic question 'Why ought I (or anyone) act morally at all?' Once one *assumes* a moral dimension to human life (i.e. assumes that men do have duties), it is a comparatively easy matter to formulate a theory that elaborates these duties. But it is the original assumption that the criticism attacks, on the grounds that it is gratuitous. This assumption cannot be defended because the question 'Why ought one to be moral?' is logically unanswerable. Any attempt to answer it inevitably falls into either one of two traps. If one tries to justify morality by appealing to non-moral considerations, his attempted justification breaks down because any arguments he uses will necessarily involve a *non sequitur*. For an 'ought' can be derived only from another 'ought'. If, on the other hand, one tries to justify morality on moral grounds, he must either beg the question or become entrapped in an infinite regress.

My reply to this criticism is that my theory escapes between the horns of this traditional dilemma of moral justification. I shall not go into detail on this point here because I have already done so in Part II but simply summarize the method I have used to solve the problem. My argument proceeds from a conception of what it means to live a moral life. If the interpretation I gave of moral action – that it concerns the socially significant acts a person does and, in particular, the reasons he has for doing these acts – is sound, I am justified in concluding, as I did, that one ought never to act arbitrarily. And if a critic persists in asking 'Why ought one never to act arbitrarily?' I need only point out again that arbitrary action is irrational action, under certain specified conditions. One ought not to act arbitrarily because one ought not to act irrationally. At this point a shift occurs in the character of the argument. For the prohibition against irrational action is not moral but logical (the notion of 'action' being now given a broader meaning). By showing that the moral 'ought' is a specification of the logical 'ought', applicable to the conditions under which human beings live together, I have been able to base my justification for morality on non-moral grounds without committing a *non sequitur*. But have I avoided an infinite regress? Or could a critic not continue to pursue me by asking 'Why ought one to be rational?' Elaborated, such a question can mean only 'Why ought one to accept as true what has been demonstrated to be true?'[4] But this question answers itself; one is logically obligated to accept demonstrated truths as true because the only alternative is logical self-contradiction. And as far as this obligation is concerned, the issue of one's personal desires, whatever they may be, is irrelevant; the obligation to be rational is absolute because irrationality is logically indefensible. The logical 'ought' defends itself – or, as I said in Part II, is self-justifying – hence we face no problem either of begging the question or of getting caught in an infinite regress in defending it.

My theory thus answers that perennial and generally-considered unanswerable question of moral philosophy 'Why ought I to be moral?' by subsuming it under the question 'Why ought I to be rational?' which in turn answers itself. The reason why most traditional philosophers have failed in their efforts to cope with this question is, I believe, that they have tried to answer it in the wrong way. Western ethics has ground itself into certain theoretical grooves which lead to a dead end. To provide a viable theory of the moral life, therefore, one must wrench himself out of the traditional track to pursue an entirely different route to his goal. That is what I have attempted to do in this essay.

I should like now, in conclusion, to consider briefly a few of the practical problems that we must concern ourselves with in our attempt to live a moral life. I need not repeat that it is no easy task to fulfil the demands of morality; that much should be abundantly obvious. Yet it is possible to over-emphasize the responsibilities that we have to shoulder. Since it may seem that I have on occasion earlier in the essay myself done this and, as a result, presented an unduly severe picture of man's practical moral situation, perhaps I ought to balance the scales a bit. Morality, I have argued, requires that we deliberate before we act, if what we may do will have social effects, reaching a decision only after we have reviewed and evaluated the consequences of the alternative acts we might perform to the welfare of everyone who might be affected by our choice. But such a requirement, strictly interpreted, throws a burden on us that we cannot reasonably bear. If everyone were to deliberate in the manner I have suggested before he committed himself to act, the pace of human life would slow to a crawl. Fortunately, we do not have to do so. For we possess general guidelines, developed through man's long experience, to which we can turn to aid us in reaching our moral decisions. As John Stuart Mill speaking to the same point so aptly remarked in his *Utilitarianism*: 'Nobody argues that the art of navigation is not founded on astronomy, because sailors cannot wait to calculate the Nautical Almanack. Being rational creatures, they go to sea with it already calculated.' So, too, with all who sail.

Nevertheless, although we need not turn every practical decision we make into an agonizing personal mental and moral struggle, it remains true that we ought to be able to defend our decisions, including even those that we have made in the most routine way. In what terms, then, should such a defence be made? Since our duties are determined by the consequences of what we do, we must be able to show that we had good reason to assume that the act we decided to perform would lead to certain results. But what kind of results? First, an equal distribution of happiness and, secondly, the greatest amount of happiness possible. The primary practical task that we must all face, when we deliberate about what we ought to do, or defend some act we have done, is to balance these two factors against each other. Should I do an act that will result in equal treatment for all concerned or a different act that will produce more happiness, but only for certain ones at the expense of others? To answer this question I must put myself in the place of those whose interests would be sacrificed by the second act and decide whether I would, in their situation, be willing to waive my equal right to happiness. Only if I can honestly give an affirmative answer to this question can I consider myself morally free to choose that alternative. Since any such conclusion rests on judgments involving imponderables, no line of demarcation can be drawn that will guide us infallibly to a correct decision about what we ought to do. We must simply do our best, using our imagination, and drawing on our own experience and that of mankind as a whole.

But another practical question can be raised. I have repeatedly said that we all have a moral obligation to act in a way that will *promote* an equal amount of happiness for all those who will be affected by what we do. But how does one go about 'promoting' the happiness of someone else? Is that even possible or may my expression not be misleadingly ambitious? I think our answer must be a qualified one. The phrase 'promoting the happiness of another' does to some extent accurately describe what people in fact do. Particularly in our relationships with our intimate associates – our families and close friends – most of us perform acts that are aimed directly to the end of making someone else happy. In such cases it is fair to say that we are attempting to promote their happiness by what we do. More generally, however, we pursue our goal in a less direct way. We do things that will, we hope, secure the conditions we believe necessary to another's achievement of happiness. Examples are obvious: We try to earn a comfortable living for our family, we purchase insurance for their security, we sacrifice to enable our children to get the best possible education, and so on. Going on to consider our relationships with our fellow-men in general, it is evident that we must go about the task of promoting their happiness largely by an indirect rather than a direct route. For what could I do directly to promote the happiness of a peasant in inner China? Again, the method we ordinarily employ is to make some contribution to the conditions that we – or, more often, our society – believe to be most effective in increasing the happiness of such people. In our complex impersonal world these conditions are predominantly economic in nature. We pay taxes and our government buys grain to feed the hungry masses of Asia.

There is, thus, an important link between the moral life of the individual and the economic organization and activities of society as a whole. Furthermore, the theory I have presented suggests a more specific – and, perhaps, controversial – relationship between morality and economics. If it be true that everyone has an equal right to happiness and if it be reasonable to assume that financial resources are among the most vital conditions normally necessary for the realization of happiness, then it would seem to follow that we all have a moral obligation to promote economic egalitarianism. Our acceptance of inequalities in wealth among individuals could be justified on only two grounds: (1) That some persons require more financial resources to be happy than others do (almost surely true in individual cases but equally certainly specious when employed as a generalization to justify economic inequality in a society as a whole) or (2) that those who are poor acquiesce in their poverty on grounds of self-interest, because they recognize that they are better off than they would be if everyone in society were economically equal (an argument that – according to my theory – is morally acceptable, *if* the acquiescence of those who suffer from the inequality can be successfully established).

The theory of the moral life I have presented in this essay has, moreover, implications elsewhere than simply in economics. The relationships among individuals in any society – and particularly in our complex modern world – are vast in scope and interwoven into countless intricate patterns. For a society to function successfully, institutions and agencies have to be established to direct and control these relationships. The main consequence is the development of government, whose activities range ever more widely and deeply into the lives of the citizenry. Inevitably these activities result in inequities of treatment. Because this is true, political power, if it is to be justified morally, must be exercised with the consent, either actual or tacit, of those on whom it is imposed. Political theorists have recognized as much and the doctrine of government by consent has become a canon of the democratic tradition. One of the implications of my theory is to provide an explanation and justification, on moral grounds, for the democratic principle of government by consent. Whenever possible, such consent must be actual, tacit consent being justifiable only as a substitute, necessitated by the conditions of the situation, for actual consent. Therefore, democracy, in some sense, is the only form of government that is morally defensible. However, there are many forms that a morally viable democracy might take. Whether the will of the populace is exercised through universal suffrage or by some different means is immaterial – as long as that will is expressed and functions as the guide to governmental actions. Any government, on the contrary, which forces its will on the populace without their consent and against their desires forfeits its claim to moral sanction.

The views I have just expressed regarding economics and politics have been put in very broad terms; a full analysis of these institutions would have to develop the points I have made in detail and consider a host of subsidiary questions. Since such a task would be far beyond the scope of my essay, I shall not attempt it but shall instead limit myself to a single but important point. All social institutions – economic systems, governments, educational organizations, religious bodies, and so on – are means whose function is to serve the ends of society. These ends finally are moral, consisting in the happiness that is to be realized by the people who make up the society, measured both in its quantity and its distribution. Hence the theory that I have presented in this essay has implications that encompass the whole range of our social institutions. For if it is sound, it provides a way both of morally justifying (to the extent that they are justifiable) our institutions and also, because these are a means to an end it has formulated, of establishing a criterion that can guide us in determining the form that our various institutions should most properly assume.

The activities of social institutions are, however, simply the combined and hence magnified activities of individual human beings. The crux of the moral life, thus, turns on the way in which we, as individuals, live. I would like to end my essay on this theme, by making a few remarks about the results that would follow if we were all to live as morally we ought. I shall, in other words, sketch a brief picture of the ideal society, insofar as it is realizable through the efforts of mankind.

My first comment must be (at least in part) a negative one. By an ideal society I do not mean a perfect society. Even if, what we can never expect, everyone were to live a thoroughly moral life, the ills of human existence would by no means be completely eradicated. For conscientiousness alone, even when informed by correct moral principles, is not sufficient to realize the ends toward which it is aimed. In addition, we need intelligence to determine correctly what those ends are and control over our environment to make their realization possible. I said earlier in the essay that the development of science and technology enlarges our moral obligations; I can add here that, by the same token, it increases our ability successfully to fulfil them. But beyond such possibilities, the unfortunate fact remains that the universe contains forces that adversely affect the happiness of mankind over which we have little or no control. Although man has by his intelligence and industry gradually built walls to repel some of these hostile natural forces, there is little hope that he can ever conquer them. Hence the vision of a perfect human society will probably always remain vain. Nevertheless, men can by their own activities improve the societies in which they live. And moral activity, I should argue, is one of the methods necessary to realize whatever improvement is possible. Indeed, if everyone were to combine in his actions the conscientiousness demanded by morality with the intelligence allotted to most of us and the control over our environment made possible by science and technology, the society that would emerge would be, in comparison to any existent society, truly ideal.

About the lives men would live in such a society we can say, first, that these will be moral and, secondly, that they will be as happy as the vicissitudes of human existence allow. I have written much in this essay about human life in terms of its moral requirements, less about it in terms of its possible happiness. The two sides are, however, obviously linked. So it might seem that this would be an appropriate place for me to paint in the brightest colours I could imagine a picture of the happiness that we should all enjoy in an ideal society. But I will forego the endeavour, mainly because I doubt that any palette could hold all the colours needed. Or, to descend from the realm of metaphor, I have doubts about any generalizations I might make concerning the kinds of life in which men will find their happiness. I emphasize this point because philosophers and social reformers alike have exhibited a prediliction for stipulating the activities in which alone men can realize their *true* happiness. As a result, their ideal societies sometimes more resemble vast machines composed of mutually replaceable parts than communities of human beings. I believe, on the contrary, that among the most valuable aspects of human nature is its diversity. Individuals should be encouraged to seek their happiness in widely different pursuits and modes of life. In any society that I could call ideal, each member would follow his own best path to happiness, however far it might wander from the paths followed by his fellows, as long as none of these paths was pursued at the expense of the happiness of anyone else.

We all seek to be happy; we all ought to be moral. To satisfy both often appears to us impossible. Yet some individuals have apparently achieved in a high degree a life that combines the two. To what extent the ideal is realizable is, perhaps, a question that each person must answer for his own life. But what more could one wish to have said of him than 'There goes a good and happy man'?

NOTES TO PART IV

[1] It might be noted that John Stuart Mill's version of hedonism is less objective than that of Bentham. By insisting on qualitative differences in pleasures Mill introduced a factor into our moral decisions that is not easily amenable to quantification and mathematical computation. This left him with the problem of how to determine the relative quality of different pleasures, a problem he solved in the following way: 'Of two pleasures, if there be one to which all or almost all who have experience of both give a decided preference, irrespective of any feeling of moral obligation to prefer it, that is the more desirable pleasure' (*Utilitarianism*). In its appeal to personal preference Mill's theory clearly introduces a subjective element that Bentham's avoids.

[2] Other forms of subjectivism that have been prevalent in Western philosophy include the views that, to decide what we ought to do, we should consult our feelings, our sentiments, our will, our 'moral sense', and so on. To the objection that a conscience theorist might make against my classification of his rule of action as subjective, I would reply that I am using the term 'subjective' in a specific, limited sense. In that sense it clearly does apply to his rule. Furthermore, as I shall go on to argue, this subjectivity of his rule precludes the possibility of its being objective in the sense in which most conscience theorists would claim it to be.

[3] I should note that the issue I am concerned with here is limited to the question: Can we justify our belief that a certain act is our duty by appealing to our conscience? I do not consider the question of the moral character of an agent who follows the dictates of his conscience, wherever they may lead. This issue raises interesting, important, and extremely difficult problems which, however, lie outside the scope of the present essay.

[4] I might note here, what should be apparent, that anyone who expects an answer to this question in *moral* terms has failed to understand the logic of my argument. I do not maintain that we have a moral obligation to be rational – except, of course, in situations in which our acts have social consequences. Rather, the obligation involved is of a different kind.

INDEX

Aristotle, 31 ff., 45, 59
Axiological tradition, 15, 17
Bentham, J., 33, 91, 95, 97, 106
Categorical Imperative, 13
Christian theology, 23
Egalitarianism, 102
Equal Rights, Principle of, 61 ff.
Ethical egoism, 49 ff.
Ethical nihilism, 22, 94
Ethical scepticism, 22 ff.
Ethics of Aristotle, 31
Ethics of conscience, 91 ff.
Golden Mean, 13
Hedonism, 33, 44, 91, 95, 97 f., 106
Hedonistic calculus, 91, 97
Hume, D., 14, 17, 25

Intuitionism, 18 ff., 84 f., 89
Kant, I., 24
Mandeville, B., 50
Mao Tze-Tung, 70
Mill, J. S., 100, 106
Moral cynicism, 23
Newton, I., 78
Personal Impartiality, Principle of, 46 ff., 53 ff., 61 f., 64, 75 ff., 97 f.
Prichard, H. A., 10 ff., 17 f., 24 f., 36
Ross, W. D., 25
Treatise of Human Nature, 14
Utilitarianism, 14 ff., 65, 91, 100, 106
Utility, Principle of, 13, 98

GEORGE ALLEN & UNWIN LTD

Head Office
40 Museum Street, London W.C.1
Telephone: 01-405 8577

Sales, Distribution and Accounts Departments
Park Lane, Hemel Hempstead, Herts.
Telephone: 0442 3244

Athens: 34 Panepistimiou Street
Auckland: P.O. Box 36013, Northcote Central N.4
Barbados: P.O. Box 222, Bridgetown
Beirut: Deeb Building, Jeanne d'Arc Street
Bombay: 103/5 Fort Street, Bombay 1
Buenos Aires: Escritorio 454–459, Florida 165
Calcutta: 285J Bepin Behari Ganguli Street, Calcutta 12
Cape Town: 68 Shortmarket Street
Hong Kong: 105 Wing On Mansion, 26 Hancow Road, Kowloon
Ibadan: P.O. Box 62
Karachi: Karachi Chambers, McLeod Road
Madras: 2/18 Mount Road, Madras
Mexico: Villalongin 32, Mexico 5, D.F.
Nairobi: P.O. Box 30583
Philippines: P.O. Box 157, Quezon City D-502
Rio de Janeiro: Caixa Postal 2537-Zc-00
Singapore: 36c Prinsep Street, Singapore 7
Sydney N.S.W.: Bradbury House, 55 York Street
Tokyo: C.P.O. Box 1728, Tokyo 100–91
Toronto: 81 Curlew Drive, Don Mills

GIDON ALAIN GUY GOTTLIEB
The Logic of Choice

This is a critical study of the concept of 'rule' used in law, ethics and much philosophical analysis which the author uses to investigate the concept of 'rationality'. The author indicates in what manner the modes of reasoning involved in reliance upon rules are unique and in what fashion they provide an alternative both to the modes of logico-mathematical reasoning and to the modes of scientific reasoning. He thus prepares the groundwork for a methodology meeting the requirements of the fields using rules such as law and ethics. He utilizes current examples drawn from English and American legal decisions to suggest how the positions of legal positivism and of natural law are equally artificial and misleading.

The author also discusses other substantive issues related to the mainstream of legal philosophy—theories of interpretation, the notion of purpose and the requirements of principled decision-making.

ALBERT SCHWEITZER
Civilization and Ethics

The whole history of civilization as Dr Schweitzer sees it, is a struggle towards an ethical outlook on life. Without such an outlook, or if it is insecurely held, civilization decays. As he reviews the course of Western philosophy down to our own time, he shows just how we have come to be left without a mora leg to stand on. But unlike so many writers who reach similarly gloomy conclusions, Dr Schweitzer is ready to build afresh, on his famous principle of 'reverence for life', a positive philosophy with which to meet the problems of today. His idealism demands that each individual should acknowledge 'responsibility without limit to all that lives'.

BERTRAND RUSSELL
Authority and the Individual

In an ever more complex and dangerous world, planning, prudence and control—all the authoritarian virtues—become ever more necessary if anarchy and destruction are to be avoided. Yet for the individual, with his need for spontaneity and a touch of glory, they spell increasing spiritual death. How can the two be reconciled? Bertrand Russell discusses the origins of human institutions and the areas where control is appropriate, if widely shared, and those where, if we are to avoid listlessness and stagnation, individual initiative must be allowed free play. The book consists of the BBC Reith Lectures for 1948, the first to be delivered in this distinguished series. Like most of Russell's works, it is as much, if not more, to the point today than when it first appeared.

Marriage and Morals

By what code do we live our sexual lives? A new morality less distorting to human personality but nonetheless careful of social needs, in keeping with the emancipation of women and the development of contraceptives, was advocated by Bertrand Russell thirty years ago. Are we now living it? Or has conventional morality largely kept its hold?

Whatever one's ideas on the subject they can hardly fail to be clarified by this examination of it. Every aspect, from the origin of marriage to the value of a healthy sex life, from the influence of religion to the possibilities of eugenics, receives the incisive scrutiny of Bertrand Russell's intellect. Here is the Passionate Sceptic at his most vigorous.

R. S. PETERS
Ethics and Education

If ever there was a time when fundamental work was required in the philosophy of education, it is the present. Education has become a matter of grave public concern. Demands for its extension and plans for its reorganization abound. It has become rather like the kingdom of Heaven in former times. It is both within us and amongst us, yet it also lies ahead. The elect possess it and hope to gather in those who are not yet saved. But what education is is seldom clear.

A fundamental task of philosophy has always been to clarify our concepts, to answer the Socratic question 'What do you mean?' This question has never been asked systematically about 'education'. Part I of this book attempts to do this and to relate the concept of 'education' here developed to what goes on in educational institutions. Even more important, however, in philosophy is the question 'How do you know?' The search for justification is particularly urgent and particularly difficult in the sphere of value. Education necessarily involves judgements of value and at the moment in England and America education is a topic which arouses moral fervour both inside and outside the profession. Education has become as moralized as marriage and politics.

Parts II and III of this book attempt to provide a proper ethical foundation for education in a democratic society. A positive ethical theory is developed which, it is hoped, will contribute to ethics in general as well as to the ethics of education.

The book is written so that it can be easily understood by the educated public, and by teachers on the job and in training as well as by students of philosophy. It does not aspire to provide simple solutions for complex problems in which issues of fact are closely intertwined with issues of value, but only to provide a clear and coherent basis in ethical theory for the discussion of such issues.

LONDON: GEORGE ALLEN AND UNWIN